Praise for *Fii*

Every once in a while, a game-ch... ... ... I believe this is one of them. In *Find More Money*, Art Rainer gives leaders who feel stuck financially some brilliant strategies that I think can change the future, not just the future of families, but the future of the kingdom. You can only cut so much. If you're ready to start adding or multiplying, this book is for you.

Carey Nieuwhof, author and founding
pastor of Connexus Church

One of the harder things of pastoring was knowing how many of our church attendees that struggled financially. Regardless of why—whether it was their fault or not—they simply were not able to find a way forward financially. Sadly, it impacted everything and everyone around them, including their desire and ability to support the mission efforts about which they were passionate. If that's your story, or you know someone who has that story, this book is for you! With *Find More Money*, Art provides another practical, easy-to-understand, yet entertaining financial book. You will actually enjoy learning how to increase your income and obtain financial health for the sake of advancing God's kingdom.

Ron Edmondson, CEO, Leadership Network,
author of *The Mythical Leader*

Art Ranier's new book, *Find More Money*, will help you to establish the right goals, provide insights on how to accomplish the right goals and the motivation to complete them. Buy it, read it and put it into practice!

Chuck Bentley, CEO, Crown.org,
author of *Money Problems, Marriage Solutions*

Without question, Art has a passion for seeing people obtain financial health for the sake of advancing God's kingdom. In *Find More Money*, Art focuses on the "other side" of the financial equation—the income side. Like his other books, *Find More Money* can be enjoyed and understood by all. If cutting your budget no longer cuts it for you, this is your book.

Rob West, president, Kingdom Advisors

Sharing Art's passion for helping believers with money, I am thrilled that he wrote *Find More Money*. The wide array of ways to increase our income is unlike any other time in history, and Art does a masterful job of practically guiding us on how to do just that. I have no doubt that God's kingdom is going to be greatly advanced by the message of this book!

Bob Lotich, founder of Seedtime.com

Praise for *The Marriage Challenge*

The Marriage Challenge is an excellent book to help couples find oneness in their finances. The story format makes the book a fun read for both the husband and wife. God has designed your marriage to showcase the gospel. Don't let financial issues get in the way of a great marriage. Read *The Marriage Challenge*!

Daniel L. Akin, president of Southeastern Baptist Theological Seminary, Wake Forest, North Carolina

I have known and worked with Art Rainer for several years and have always been encouraged by his infectious, 360-degree vision for mission in every part of life. This fuels his works on careful thinking and management of money—from personal devotion to marriage, from raising kids to leadership, the local church, education, and understanding the world. I am pleased to recommend this to you.

Keith and Kristyn Getty, modern hymn writers, authors of *Sing!: How Worship Transforms Your Life, Family, and Church*

Art Rainer is the new voice in personal finance for Christians. His writings and podcasts are awakening believers to grasp more completely God's plan for the money He has entrusted to us. His latest book, *The Marriage Challenge*, is an incredible resource for all married couples from engaged couples to newlyweds to those married for many years. Get it and apply its principles immediately!

Thom S. Rainer, president and CEO, Church Answers

Whether you are newly married or have been married for years, this book is for you! Art provides clear, practical steps toward financial health, and addresses underlying issues couples experience that present themselves in their finances. Both your marriage and your bank account will be stronger by applying the principles found in this book! Art Rainer's writing style is like having your own personal marriage and financial counselor and advisor. His personal and often entertaining approach helps to break down barriers for couples creating the opportunity for greater unity and success in their approach to money. This book is guaranteed to positively impact the reader!

Selma Wilson, former senior vice president of
LifeWay Christian Resources

Praise for *The Money Challenge*

Art has written an incredibly practical, readable, useful book on living openhandedly with our finances. *The Money Challenge* offers practical steps to live as God has designed us to: as channels of His great generosity, to advance His kingdom. I highly recommend it!

Matt Carter, pastor of preaching and vision,
The Austin Stone Community Church, Austin, Texas

I can't wait for you to read Art's book. It is so good. Art encourages and equips you in *The Money Challenge.* Not only will you learn a lot, but you will also enjoy his captivating writing style.

Derwin L. Gray, lead pastor, Transformation Church,
Indian Land, South Carolina

Sometimes the hardest part of wise financial stewardship is knowing where to start. That's where Art's book comes in—his relatable stories and practical steps break down a seemingly impossible goal to simple, faith-filled steps. Join him in this thirty-day challenge and watch as God uses this book to propel you into a lifestyle of generous giving. Around The Summit Church we always say, "Live sufficiently, give extravagantly." This is how to start.

J.D. Greear, PhD, pastor of The Summit Church,
Raleigh-Durham, North Carolina, and author of
Gaining by Losing: Why the Future Belongs to Churches that Send

The Money Challenge is a hopeful, gospel-oriented primer on using finances for the sake of the kingdom. Everyone can benefit from the biblical wisdom here, regardless of financial or social background.

Russell Moore, president, Southern Baptist
Ethics & Religious Liberty Commission

FIND MORE MONEY

INCREASE YOUR INCOME to TACKLE DEBT,
SAVE WISELY, and LIVE GENEROUSLY

FIND MORE MONEY

ART RAINER

B&H
PUBLISHING
NASHVILLE, TENNESSEE

978-1-5359-7107-2

Published by B&H Publishing Group
Nashville, Tennessee

Dewey Decimal Classification: 248.6
Subject Heading: CHRISTIAN LIFE /
STEWARDSHIP / TIME MANAGEMENT

1 2 3 4 5 6 • 24 23 22 21 20

To my brothers, Sam and Jess.
I love you guys.

Acknowledgments

As any author knows, producing a book takes a team. Behind the lone name on the cover are a host of people working hard to get a book into the hands of those who need it. So to everyone involved, I am incredibly grateful for you.

To my wife, Sarah, thank you for your love and support. Thank you for sacrificially caring for our boys. Most importantly, thank you for putting your love for Jesus and others on full display. I am blessed because you are my wife.

To Nathaniel, Joshua, and James, you all bring me such happiness. I love you. I am proud of you. And I am glad that you are my sons.

To the rest of the family—the Rainers, Dues, and Halls. Thank you for your continued encouragement. Dad and Mom, I love you.

To the Southeastern Baptist Theological Seminary family, I love being on mission with you all. I thank God that I get to work alongside such Great Commission-minded men and women. Rachel Lambert and Amy Whitfield, your involvement with this book was invaluable.

To the B&H team, thank you for your work and ministry. Devin Maddox, Taylor Combs, and Jenaye White—I could not have asked for a better group.

To those who shared their side gig story, thank you for inviting others in, encouraging readers to find more money and advance God's kingdom.

Of course, I am grateful for my Lord and Savior, Jesus Christ. I don't deserve the gift I have received. The gifts of grace, mercy, and kindness God has freely given me are overwhelming. I don't understand why such a holy God would save such a sinner like me.

Contents

Yesterday

It was Saturday. A half-eaten chocolate and vanilla marble cake sat on the round kitchen table. White plastic cups were sporadically perched on counters, bookshelves, the microwave, and, of course, on the table next to the marble cake. Eight pink and light-blue helium-filled balloons still levitated above the chair to which they were anchored. Shards of light-blue confetti littered the apartment's den carpet.

Brooklyn was pregnant with a boy. He was their first child.

Yesterday was a day of celebration. Yesterday happiness-infused shrieks resounded. Yesterday glee-induced tears trickled down a new mom's cheek. Yesterday elation elevated everyone, as men and women jumped up and down.

Yesterday there was laughter, hugs, and high fives. Yesterday family and friends crowded the modest two-bedroom townhouse.

Yesterday was a good day.

But that was yesterday.

Today is different.

Today it's quiet in the townhouse, located just outside Raleigh, North Carolina. The only sounds are coming from the hum of the overhead fan and an occasional car driving down the street behind their humble backyard. Austin and Brooklyn sit next to each other on their small, navy couch. With one hand Austin holds Brooklyn's. With the other he holds a piece of paper. Never before have the young couple been so filled with excitement and yet, so paradoxically, filled with fear.

"What are we going to do?" questions Brooklyn, searching Austin's face for some form of reassurance. All she finds is an expressionless daze.

Today Austin and Brooklyn are still excited about having a son. That hasn't changed. But another reality brought along a new competing emotion.

The opening of a bill sometimes seems mundane. The envelope is torn, and the bill is removed from its encasing. After a quick glance at the bill, the piece of paper is often set aside to be paid later that day or week.

But the opening of this bill was anything but mundane for Austin and Brooklyn. The event was not ordinary but nerve-racking. The opening of the bill that Austin now held turned a knot inside his stomach and brought a different kind of tears to Brooklyn's eyes, tears not motivated by overwhelming happiness but tremendous concern. There was no quick glance at the bill, just a long solemn stare.

Austin finally answered Brooklyn's question, but it wasn't what Brooklyn wanted to hear, and it wasn't what Austin wanted to say.

"I don't know. I just don't know."

Austin and Brooklyn feared this day would come, but they kept hoping that somehow their finances would work out, that everything would be okay.

But everything was not okay. And this bill made that reality abundantly clear.

"We're broke," said Austin with a deep sigh.

Again words Brooklyn would rather not hear, especially now that they had a baby on the way.

"We can't pay this," continued Austin. "We don't have any more money."

Austin let go of Brooklyn's hand, holding the bill with both hands. He leaned forward, studying the paper, looking for something, anything, to help but knowing he would find nothing.

He set the bill down on the coffee table in front of them.

Austin shook his head. "We just can't do this anymore."

Brooklyn wanted to disagree, but she couldn't. Austin was right. They could not do this anymore. Something had to change.

Find more money.
Get financially healthy.
Advance God's kingdom.

When Cutting Your Budget No Longer Cuts It

Austin and Brooklyn seemed like the ideal couple. In some ways they were. Their parents had the same idea when it came to names. Austin got his name because he was born in Austin, Texas. And Brooklyn got her name because she was born in Brooklyn, New York.

They met in college while serving at their church. Austin and Brooklyn were some of the courageous few who dared to serve in the middle school ministry, and it wasn't long after they met that they started dating.

They loved God, ministry, and each other. The couple married the summer after college graduation.

Austin had a strong desire to one day be a pastor. After Austin and Brooklyn were married, they both went to seminary and got degrees that would help them serve a local church.

Upon graduating from seminary, a small church outside of Raleigh, Little Creek Community Church, asked Austin if he would be their youth pastor, ministering to the church's middle and high school students. The church was unable to pay Austin much, but he and Brooklyn decided to make it work.

They fell in love with Little Creek. Austin was the only one getting paid, but like many ministry couples, both he and Brooklyn poured their lives into the teenagers. Brooklyn found part-time work as a substitute teacher, and though they had some student loans and credit card debt, they bought a fixer-upper townhouse in an unassuming area close to the church. They figured it was better to buy than to rent. Plus, Austin was a pretty good handyman. He had already helped a few friends renovate their houses. Austin and Brooklyn figured he could do the same thing with their townhouse.

The two of them made the finances work for about three years. Every month was tight, but they made it, rarely eating out and paying only the minimum amount required on their credit cards and student loans. After giving to the church and paying their bills, there was little to no room for savings or putting more money toward debt, but they were getting by.

And then last month happened.

Brooklyn had to go to the doctor a few different times. Up until this point, Austin and Brooklyn had been able to avoid the doctor and medical bills. But with a baby on the way, they understandably did not want to risk the health of baby or mother.

Sitting on the couch, holding a medical bill they could not pay, they realized that caring for their physical health had crushed any hope of financial health unless something changed.

"We can't move forward like this," said a frustrated Austin. "We're almost thirty, have no savings, no retirement, debt, and can't afford our own son."

Brooklyn added, "The doctor's office said we should expect to pay around $7,500 to have our son delivered."

"I know, Brooklyn," fumed Austin with a raised voice. "I know we don't have any money, and I know what they said. I was there with you!"

Austin didn't mean to snap at Brooklyn, but he did.

Brooklyn was taken aback by Austin's response. Arguments were rare for the couple. Feeling attacked, Brooklyn stood up and snapped back.

"Look, don't get angry at me because you took a low-paying job!"

Austin yelled, "We could probably make it if you didn't want to give away so much of our income to the church!"

Austin didn't mean that. He loved Brooklyn's desire to live generously, and he saw the impact of their generosity in their church firsthand. He needed to keep a level head about this. But he needed to act quickly.

"I think I need to resign from Little Creek," he said.

Brooklyn's stomach dropped. She didn't like the thought. And she knew Austin didn't either. They loved their little church. They didn't want to leave it.

Brooklyn sat back down next to Austin. She put her arm around him and laid her head on his shoulder.

Austin let out a sigh. "We don't have any more expenses to cut. We just need to find more money."

"Try not to think about it right now," said Brooklyn calmly. "We need to get ready for church tomorrow."

The $1.19 Meal

I had known John casually for a few years. He was a good guy. Though we'd had prior conversations, this was the first time we talked about money (which is weird considering how much I talk and write about the topic).

John asked if we could meet about his finances. He wanted to develop habits that would set him up for future financial health. He wanted to start giving and saving more. I was proud of him for wanting this, and I was happy to help.

But John had a problem. There was never any money left in his bank account. He had a budget, but since he could not save or give, he assumed something was wrong with it.

He handed me his budget. "Can you help me?" he asked.

I looked over it for about fifteen seconds. There really wasn't much to it.

"So, this is it for you?" I asked.

He nodded.

"Well, your issue is pretty easy to diagnose," I said.

"Great," he responded.

"You need to reduce your food budget," I said with a grin.

John was not laughing. He didn't seem to know what to say.

"I'm joking."

John's food budget was $50. The USDA says that a "thrifty" food budget is around $43 per week for a guy like John. So, John's budget was pretty much on track, right? Wrong. John didn't budget $50 per week. He budgeted $50 for every two weeks. That comes to $1.19 per meal, assuming he was eating three meals per day (I should note that John was single).

John didn't need to cut his food budget. He really didn't need to cut any of his expenses. He couldn't. There was nothing to cut because there was no more meat on the bone.

John didn't have an expense issue. He had an income issue.

The Disappearance of Margin

Since you are reading this book, you probably already know and live this—Americans struggle in the area of personal finances.

Forty percent of Americans cannot cover a $400 financial emergency.[1] They are not able to pull together $400 in cash from their checking account, savings account, or under their mattress.

Those who have credit card debt average around $15,000 of it.[2] The average yearly interest paid on these credit cards is more than $1,100.

Forty-four percent of American adults have car loans.[3] And as car prices climb, Americans are opting for longer term loans, which reduces the monthly payment but also makes the loan more expensive. Leases account for approximately 30 percent of new car "purchases."

Student loan debt has become the second largest debt type in America, behind mortgages.[4] College graduates now leave college with a degree and an average of $37,000 in student loan debt. This debt causes young adults to delay common milestones, like buying a house.

You may think debt and a lack of savings are young adult problems and assume that, over time, things will work themselves out. Unfortunately this is not true. The bankruptcy rate for those over the age of sixty-five increased by 204 percent from 1991 to 2018.[5] Retirees regularly say that running out of money is one of their greatest financial concerns.

One of the primary reasons why so many people struggle to get out of these situations is that margin has disappeared from our finances.

Margin is the cushion in our finances—what we have left over after we give generously, save wisely, and live appropriately. Margin is what allows you to put additional money toward debt. Margin is what allows you to give more when God prompts your heart. Margin is what allows you to make sure bills are paid without a problem.

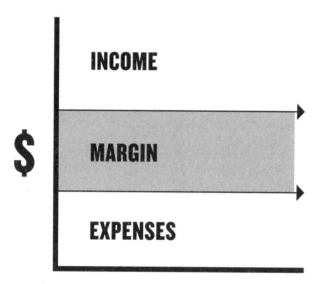

But most people don't have financial leftovers. Seventy-eight percent of Americans live paycheck to paycheck.[6] That means almost four out of every five of us are living on the financial edge. Just one unforeseen cost can push most over the edge.

We all need margin in our budgets. We need financial space to give generously and save wisely. We need financial space to pay off our debts. We need financial space to save for retirement. And often we're looking to create this space on the wrong side of the financial equation.

The Forgotten Side of the Financial Equation

A pastor without Social Security and savings is facing retirement. A middle-aged, sixty-hour-a-week air-conditioner repairman is figuring out how to pay for his daughter's college. A millennial is struggling because her salary doesn't provide enough to pay down her college loans.

Just reduce your expenses to create margin, right?

Maybe.

When someone says they struggle with their finances, they are usually presented a remedy that deals with their expenses:

Reduce your spending.

Downsize your home.

Stop eating out so much.

Don't go to Disney World twice a year (Sorry, Mickey).

Don't send your child to an outrageously expensive private
    college.

Purchase generic label items.

Get rid of your Netflix subscription.

Don't buy a new car.

All of these can be helpful. Getting your expenses under control can help you give more and save more. They can create margin in your budget.

If . . .

If your problem is only on the expense side of the financial equation.

You see, while we often focus on the expense side of the financial equation, we forget that there is another side. The other side plays an incredibly important role in one's financial well-being.

On one side you have expenses.

But on the other side you have income, the money you make.

INCOME | EXPENSES

Over the years I've had several conversations with people about their financial health. They want to follow God's design for their money. They want to give generously, save wisely, and live appropriately. They long to find themselves in a place where they can live the generous life God created them to live for the sake of his kingdom.

Often I tell them to crush their debt or to reduce their spending. Because that's what is preventing their financial health. They have an expense issue.

But there are times when neither of those solutions will work or, at least, not on their own. These people were living paycheck to paycheck. They were part of the 78 percent who have no money left at the end of each month. Some didn't have any credit card debt. Some had credit card debt but no additional money to put toward it; they couldn't reduce expenses by magically making their debt payments disappear. Some couldn't downsize their homes; their houses were small, and their payments were already low. Some truly couldn't reduce spending; their budgets were bare bones.

Like John, they didn't have an expense issue. They had an income issue.

You may be like John as well. It never seems like you can get ahead financially. You try to follow all of the steps we "financial gurus" tell you to take, but none of it really works for you. Because sometimes the focus doesn't just need to be on the expenses.

The good news is that this book is written for people just like you. It is for those who find themselves living paycheck to paycheck, financially struggling each month and yet unable to reduce expenses or put more money toward killing debt. It's just not an option. You need more money.

You need more money just to make it through each month.

You need more money so you can pay down your debt.

You need more money so you can create an emergency savings account.

You need more money so you can eventually retire.

You need more money so you can be more generous.

Does everyone need more money? No. But do some? Absolutely.

This book will focus on what many personal finance books leave out, the forgotten side of the equation—the income side.

Don't Quit Your Job

How can you find more money? How can you increase the income side of your financial equation? When considering how you can make more money, there are three primary options.

Option 1: Get a raise.

Option 2: Get a new job.

Option 3: Get a side gig.

When most people think about increasing their income, their mind races to option 1 and option 2. They try to figure out whether they can get a raise or find a new job that will pay more. And these are valid options. But what if neither of those options is a reality?

One of the groups of people for whom I have a great burden are those in full-time ministry. Some are pastors, and some hold other types of ministry positions. These men and women sacrifice a lot for the sake of ministering to others, including their finances. For most, ministry is not a lucrative career choice. It's consistently rated as one of the worst financial returns on education. Ministers don't do it for money, and they don't do it for prestige. They do it because they love God and people.

When I wrote *The Money Challenge*, I was approached by many in ministry. They told me about their financial struggles. For some the answer was on the expense side, so that book helped them. But for others it was not.

Many of them clearly needed to find more money. They were struggling to get by on their salaries. And it wasn't their churches' fault. Their churches wanted to pay them more but couldn't.

"I don't want to leave the church, but I need to care for my family. What I am supposed to do?" I received that general question over and over again.

And I want to give you the same advice I gave them.

You don't always have to quit your job to increase your income. Sometimes, you just need a side gig.

The Gig Economy and You

The way we make money is changing.

Working a nine-to-five job is still prevalent in our economy, but it's losing its grip. There are more ways to make a buck than working a traditional job.

You might be familiar with the word *gig*. Historically, *gig* referred to a live musical performance. Getting a gig was a big deal for a new band: "Hey, we got our first gig!" It was an agreement for a one-time event, no strings attached. The band played, the venue owner paid, and the band went home. That was a gig.

The concept of a gig, a short-term agreement, now extends well beyond the music industry. Gig economy workers are all around us.

About one-third of U.S. workers are a part of the gig economy; that's approximately 57 million people.[7] The prevalence of short-term contracts, independent contracts, and freelancing has produced what we call the gig economy. These workers find income outside the typical long-term worker-employer relationship.

In this book we will use the term *side gig* frequently. The term assumes you have a regular, full-time job. The gig is something you do on the side.

Why do people want to dive into the gig economy? One survey found that 68 percent of side-giggers simply wanted to make more money. Sound familiar? They viewed project-to-project work as a viable way to make additional income.

"But I don't want to drive for Uber!"

I hear you. But if you think participating in the gig economy means you must drive for a ride-share service, you may have a limited understanding of the opportunities presented in the gig economy. And that's okay. We'll talk about that later.

"But I am not a techie!"

Again I hear you. Many people associate the gig economy with technology. Certainly technology has played a tremendous role in accelerating the prevalence of side gig work. But you don't have to create a smartphone app to have a side gig. As you will see later, a side gig is sometimes helped by technology but does not always require it.

"But I'm too old for this."

Okay, now you're just trying to find a way out of it! Yes, right now, those participating in the gig economy are mostly young. Millennials are the most likely generation to participate in the gig economy. But older generations are jumping in as well. Thirty-two percent of people older than thirty-five are making money in the gig economy. There are opportunities out there for a wide range of ages.

Benefits of Getting a Gig

Of course side gigs require time and effort, but there are plenty of reasons millions are getting gigs. There are benefits to side gigs that often aren't available in the traditional work world.

Schedule Flexibility

Many side gigs allow you to set your own schedule. This is big for those with full-time jobs. They're able to work around the full-time, traditional job or any other activities they deem important.

Job Flexibility

By their nature, gigs are not permanent. You are not stuck with a particular gig for the rest of your life. For many gigs, you can start and stop work as you please. This also means you can find another gig if you don't like your current one. Gig-hopping is a regular occurrence. Now this doesn't mean there's no value in staying with a gig over long periods of time. We will talk about that later.

Creative Freedom

Many gigs allow you to express your creativity more freely than you can in traditional jobs. This is especially true if you choose to start your own business.

Additional Income

It's why you picked up this book. Gigs provide a way to increase your income when asking for a raise or finding a higher paying job just doesn't work out. Many are finding gigs that help them meet their financial goals. And you can too.

Average Can Be Extraordinary

The average side-gigger makes $8,000 per year.[8]

What can average do?

Since the average amount of credit card debt is $15,000, an average person could be free of credit card debt in approximately two years.

An average person could infuse $8,000 into their annual budget, ensuring that bills are paid.

An average person could max out their Roth IRA contribution, $6,000, every year.

Not bad for average.

What if you could have margin in your budget?

What if you could give more?

What if you could pay down your debt?

What if you could set aside money for an emergency?

What if you could set aside money for retirement?

What if you could live more generously?

What if you could get financially healthy for the sake of impacting eternity?

You can.

You can find more money. And just being average can substantially impact your financial health.

You are about to be introduced to your nine-step, *Find More Money* workflow that will serve as your guide. You are about to start your journey to find more money.

You can do this. And it starts with understanding God's design for money and work.

Your *Find More Money* Workflow

Workflow—sequential steps to help you reach your goal.

This is your *Find More Money* Workflow:

- ❏ Step 1: Know God's Plan for Money
- ❏ Step 2: Know God's Plan for Work
- ❏ Step 2: Know Your Find More Money Goal
- ❏ Step 3: Know You
- ❏ Step 4: Know Your Opportunity
- ❏ Step 5: Get a Gig
- ❏ Step 6: Know Your Business
- ❏ Step 7: Get Organized
- ❏ Step 8: Overcommunicate
- ❏ Step 9: Create Fans

Now, let's get to work.

Find more money.
Get financially healthy.
Advance God's kingdom among the lost.

Know God's Plan for Money

Something's wrong," said Cary.

It was Sunday and church had just concluded. Austin was outside on the church steps, greeting familiar faces as they exited. The warmth of the noon, spring sun was a welcome change from an abnormally cold winter.

Cary and his wife Marilyn were Austin's best volunteers. Cary managed a hardware store and was known to be incredibly generous and a great parent. When Austin found out about Brooklyn's pregnancy, he leaned into Cary's wisdom and experience. For the past several weeks, they had been meeting every Monday morning for breakfast to talk life and parenting.

Cary's daughter Sophia stood by Cary's side. Sophia was one of those impressive elementary school students who actually paid attention and took notes during the church service. Austin figured Cary must be doing something really right as a parent.

Austin looked at Cary. "What do you mean 'something's wrong'?"

Cary backed away from the church's foot traffic, Sophia still by his side. Austin followed.

"You," replied Cary. "Something's wrong with you. You haven't been the same today. What's up?"

Austin shook his head. "You're right. I've been pretty transparent with you about some of my concerns as a parent," Austin said, clearly indicating he had not shared everything. "We have some big money issues. With the baby on the way, I can't afford to work here anymore." Austin wasn't sure he wanted to let that slip on Sunday morning, but there was no going back now.

"What do you mean?"

"Brooklyn and I don't have any savings, we have no money to pay down debt, and we can't even afford to have a baby right now," answered Austin solemnly. "We really love this church, but we just can't live off the salary they provide us."

Cary silently nodded.

"Look, we don't blame Little Creek," Austin said warmly. "The church's budget is small. They do the best they can. But it isn't enough for us to pay our bills and, soon, feed our son."

Suddenly Sophia spoke up, "Give—Save—Live. That is the Master's Money Plan!" She had a big smile.

Cary smiled at his daughter. "Sophia and her friends have been learning a lot about God's design for money lately. She has three jars at home—Give, Save, Live. First give, next save, then live off what's left."

"They're called capsules, Dad," said Sophia, still smiling.

"Sure they are," grinned Cary. He patted Sophia on the back.

Austin wasn't sure how he felt about this conversation. It seemed like Cary's daughter had a better grip on her money than he did on his. But he was encouraged that a young girl like she could learn so much about God's design for money. It was another reason for him to learn from Cary.

"I'm glad you start with giving," said Austin to Sophia. "We often regret past purchases, but we never regret past generosity. Brooklyn and I give, even during tough times."

Austin meant those words. He and Brooklyn had frequent conversations about their desire to give more, but they simply could not. Their financial situation held them back.

Sophia comfortably encouraged Austin, "Pastor Austin, one time my friend wanted to give money to his school's fund-raiser. But he didn't have any, so we sold lemonade to help him raise money."

Cary put his hand on Austin's shoulder. "Before you turn in your resignation, let's meet at least one more time. Believe it or not, Sophia is on to something."

Sophia grinned.

"Okay," Austin agreed. "But I can't wait long. The baby will be here in twenty-two weeks."

"I understand," reassured Cary. "See you tomorrow. And bring lemons."

Austin couldn't tell if he was serious.

"Joking," smiled Cary.

———

God and Money

Why do you care about finding more money?
To pay your bills?
To pay off your debt?
To build your savings account?

These are all good goals. But is that where your motivation stops?

Motivations matter. The *why* matters. Look, if you get the *why* wrong, I promise the *how* won't deliver the results you ultimately want. Your soul longs for something greater than paying the bills, paying off debt, and obtaining financial health.

We all do. Because God designed us that way.

God cares about your relationship with money. Deeply. Did you know that God wove more than two thousand verses into the Bible about money, possessions, and resources? While Jesus was here on earth, he spoke about money more than any other topic. It's true. Go ahead and take a look. There's a reason—he cares deeply about how you relate to, manage, and use money.

You see, the way we relate to money and our possessions can either bring us closer to the heart of God or lure us farther away. Consider the rich young ruler in Matthew 19. He asked Jesus what he needed to do to have eternal life, an important question. Jesus told him to keep all the commands. The man claimed he had done this (which, of course, was a lie).

Jesus then told him to sell all of his possessions. The man walked away sad because he was not willing to part with his stuff. He was lured away by his possessions, physically and spiritually distancing himself from Jesus. His grip on money and possessions was symptomatic of a heart that had not yet taken hold of God. Like the parable of the sower in Matthew 13, the deceitfulness of wealth had choked out the word, the truth.

And he walked away sad.

Holding tightly to money and possessions never leads us to the things our soul truly desires.

In 1 Timothy 6:17–19, we find Paul encouraging Timothy to teach the rich something important about their relationship with money. Paul writes:

> Instruct those who are rich in the present age not to be arrogant or to set their hope on the uncertainty of wealth, but on God, who richly provides us with all things to enjoy. Instruct them to do what is good, to be rich in good works, to be generous and willing to share, storing up treasure for themselves as a good foundation for the coming age, so that they may take hold of what is truly life.

Now you may be thinking, *Art, you need another verse. Do you remember your book's title? I'm not rich; I'm reading this book because I need to make more money. Maybe you should find a verse that's talking to those who are financially struggling in the present age.*

When gauging our own wealth, we often compare ourselves to those who have more and not less. So let's consider your financial position from a different view—how the rest of the world views you.

Did you know that if you made $25,000 this past year, you are in the top 5 percent of the world's income earners? You made more than 95 percent of the world. If you made $33,000, you are in the top 1 percent of the world's income earners. You made more than 99 percent of the world.[1]

We have a really skewed view on wealth in the United States. The reality is that most of the world is looking at us like we look at Bill Gates or some other billionaire. To them, the rest of the world, we are incredibly wealthy. So congratulations! You are rich! Even if you can't pay your bills.

So Paul tells Timothy to tell rich people, like you and me, four important money lessons, lessons that, deep inside of you, you know to be true.

Money Lesson I: Place Your Hope in the Provider, Not the Provision

> ". . . not to be arrogant or to set their hope on the uncertainty of wealth, but on God, who richly provides us with all things to enjoy."

Here is what Paul is saying—*Put your hope in the Provider, not the provisions.*

Have you ever seen a landfill, where layers upon layers of trash construct a massive hill? Do you know what landfills are? Hills of past hopes. They are filled with stuff that people, including me and you, used to put their hope in. That couch you thought would bring you contentment? It's in there. That television I thought would bring me happiness? It's in there too.

Stuff is a poor hope. So is money. And you know this. Like me, you've lived it.

Making money is not unimportant. You need to pay your bills. You need to pay off your debt. You need to get financially healthy. But be careful. Those who place their ultimate hope in money end up consistently disappointed and emotionally fluctuating like the stock market. And because of the uncertainty money's hope brings, they find themselves uncertain about their present and their future, regardless of how much money is in their bank account.

More money does not lead to greater confidence in the present or future. A recent study revealed that 70 percent of those who made more than $200,000 feel stressed. This was the highest of any income category. More money, more problems.

So even while you are pursuing more income, put your hope in the one who richly provides all things, the one who is trustworthy, the one who will make good on all his promises.

Money Lesson 2: Our Response to God's Generosity Must Be Generosity

> "Instruct them to do what is good, to be rich in good works, to be generous and willing to share."

Did you catch what it means to be truly rich? In God's kingdom, being rich in possessions and money doesn't mean anything. You can be a millionaire on earth and still be considered poverty-stricken in God's kingdom. But the reverse is true as well. You can be poverty-stricken on earth but still be considered incredibly wealthy in God's kingdom.

Do you remember the story of the widow's gift? Jesus and his disciples watched as individuals gave large amounts of money to the temple. Yet Jesus said the widow who gave two small coins gave more than anyone else.

In God's economy, amount sacrificed always supersedes amount given. She was a bazillionaire in God's kingdom.

In God's economy, amount sacrificed always supersedes amount given.

I was traveling through West Virginia and came across a toll booth. I'd been through West Virginia several times, so I knew what to do. I got my $2.00 ready and rolled down the window. As I pulled up to the booth, holding out my $2.00, the attendant said something that surprised me. She said I didn't owe anything. The car in front of me had already paid my toll. Now, I didn't know who was in the car in front of me. The car was long gone anyway. So I did what you would have done—pulled the money, rolled up my window, and sped off!

I'm joking. I did what you would have really done—I handed the attendant my $2.00 and told her to cover the toll for the person behind me. I understood that I had been given something, so I gave something. My response to generosity was generosity. And it would have been for you as well.

John Newton, the man who wrote "Amazing Grace," penned these words in a letter: "The more vile we are in our own eyes, the more precious Christ will be to us." What Newton was saying was that the more we understand our sin and its consequences, the more we understand God's grace and his generosity toward us.

God has been so generous to each one of us. He gave us life. He gave us his one and only Son. And he gave us any other prosperity that we experience. And if we understand God's generosity toward us, how can we not be generous toward others?

Money Lesson 3: Preservation Depends on Destination

> ". . . storing up treasure for themselves as a good
> foundation for the coming age."

This portion of Paul's instructions comes from Jesus when he said, "Store up for yourselves treasures in heaven, where neither moth nor rust destroys, and where thieves don't break in and steal. For where your treasure is, there your heart will be also" (Matt. 6:20–21). How do you store up treasures in heaven with your earthly money? Be rich in generosity. Use it to advance God's kingdom.

No matter how much money you have in the bank, it will one day become worthless to you. And for those who put their hope in money, this realization will create despair. I love how Randy Alcorn put it:

> He who lays up treasures on earth spends his life backing away from his treasures. To him, death is loss.
>
> He who lays up treasures in heaven looks forward to eternity; he's moving daily toward his treasures. To him, death is gain.
>
> He who spends his life moving away from his treasures has reason to despair. He who spends his life moving toward his treasures has reason to rejoice.[2]

Preservation depends on destination.

Money Lesson 4: To Take Hold, You Must Let Go

And then Paul gives us the result of living and giving generously: "so that they may take hold of what is truly life."

When Paul says "truly life," he is talking about eternal life. Now, he is not saying they need to become believers. They already were. And he is not saying you can give your way to eternal life.

So, what is he saying?

Future blessings are associated with eternal life. But there are also present blessings. There are blessings in the here and now that we as believers get to experience. *If* we take hold of them. Real satisfaction, real contentment, real joy. And you know this to be true in your own life. While we frequently regret past purchases, we rarely regret past generosity.

To grasp the things of God, you must first have your hands wide open. If you have been on a high ropes course, zip line, or bungee jump, you know—to grab the experience that the course, zip line, or bungee jump has to offer, you have to let go.

And with open hands you paradoxically take hold of what is truly life, the blessings, the present blessings of eternal life—satisfaction, contentment, joy, being a part of something that is so much bigger than any of us.

Paying your bills, paying off debt, and obtaining financial health won't ultimately bring you what your soul longs for. You and I know plenty of financially healthy people who are still incredibly miserable.

To take hold, you must let go.

Let Go and Change Eternity

When was the last time you used your money in a way that brought about a sense of excitement, adventure, and satisfaction, a time you have yet to regret? I bet it was a time when you used money for something greater than yourself. You helped a family in need. You provided Christmas gifts for a child whose parents could not afford them. You gave to your church and her mission.

And you would do it all over again. Why do we experience such contentment and happiness through generosity? Why does our soul yearn to live generously?

Because our God is a generous God, and we are created in his

> **God has designed us not to be hoarders but conduits through which his generosity flows.**

image. God has designed us not to be hoarders but conduits through which his generosity flows.

But we are not to be generous just because it's a nice thing to do. There is a purpose. There is a mission. God desires for us to be generous in order to advance his kingdom. Eternal destinies are at stake.

The Great Opportunity

James Wise wrote a book titled *Inheritolatry*.[3] In it, he laid out an opportunity that we, as American Christians, possess, an opportunity that continues to burden me. I've slightly adjusted Wise's numbers, but the message remains the same.

Over the next thirty years, an estimated $30 trillion dollars will pass from one generation to the next through inheritances.[4]

Let's assume Christians make up 25 percent of our population. That means around *$7.5 trillion* will be in the hands of Christians.

Right now there are about thirty-two hundred unreached, not engaged people groups in the world, groups that have yet to hear the name of Jesus.[5] Let's assume it takes $75,000 per year to send someone to reach one group. And let's assume it takes twenty years to really engage the people group.

> 3,200 people groups x $75,000 per year x 20 years
> = $4.8 billion

In inheritances alone Christians will receive $7.5 trillion. To reach every people group in the world, we need $4.8 billion. The difference between one trillion and one billion? One trillion is equal to one thousand billion.

Let that sink in for a second. The need is a drop in the haves' bucket. *We have the resources to reach the world for Christ.*

Right now.

Pick apart the numbers all you want. The fact remains—God has given us an amazing opportunity.

But it's only amazing if we take hold of it.

And what if we don't? What if we squander it? Are we going to be the generation of Christians that cause future Christians, one hundred years from now, to wonder what we were thinking and doing? We had it in our hands! Yet we did little with it.

But what if we do?

Advancing God's kingdom—this is your and my *why.*

This is why we get out of debt.

This is why we save money.

This is why we pursue financial health.

And this is why we find more money.

Our money's priority is kingdom-advancing generosity. You're not making more money just to pay the bills, get out of debt, or save for retirement. These are good things, but they are the means, not the end. They are the means by which we can find ourselves more able to live the generous, kingdom-advancing life for which God has designed us, where we can more freely pour into our community and the world for his sake.

You thought you were just trying to make more money to pay the bills and get rid of your car loan? No, this is about something much more significant, adventurous, and satisfying than that.

The foundation upon which real, biblical financial health is established is generosity. You are trying to get financially healthy so your finances can be part of God's mission, advancing his kingdom. True financial health is living generously toward that end.

It's time to start thinking bigger. "Financial health" is just a means to a much more significant, adventure-filled, eternal end. So write down and pray for where you dream of God using your financial health to advance his kingdom.

First, consider your own church, neighborhood, city, and country. Then write down three countries other than your own.

My Church: _____

My Neighborhood: _____

My Town/City: _____

My Country: _____

Country 1: _____

Country 2: _____

Country 3: _____

Now let's do it.

Find more money.
Get financially healthy.
Advance God's kingdom among the
forgotten.

Know God's Plan for Work

The early Monday morning chill had a bite to it. It was a reminder that spring had not yet fully arrived. Winter's grip still had the morning.

Austin opened the door to the Red Spoon Diner, jingling the bells attached to the door's handle. It was a local, low-key diner, and Austin appreciated that. Cary was sitting at their usual booth, sipping a cup of black coffee. Cary always arrived a little early.

Austin sat across from Cary. The waitress placed a cup of coffee in front of him. She knew the routine well.

"What can I get you, Hon?" she asked in her thick, North Carolina accent.

"Two eggs, over easy, bacon, and toast."

"You got it, Sugar." The waitress had a ridiculous arsenal of nicknames.

She walked away to put in the order.

Cary looked at Austin. "How are you feeling?"

Austin looked down at his coffee cup for a second before answering. "Still pretty stressed. So is Brooklyn."

"I can imagine." Cary took another sip of coffee.

"We just need more margin in our budget. And I've looked at our budget. There's really nothing to it. We aren't frivolous people. I mean, I can turn off the electricity to save money, but I don't think that will go over well with Brooklyn."

Cary chuckled. "I doubt it." He sipped his coffee again. "There was a time when I was in a similar situation. Money was tight. I started as a clerk at the hardware store, and the pay wasn't great. But I liked the company, and it kept us close to family, which was important to us."

"So, what did you do?"

"Well, first I tried to change up my budget. But like you, there wasn't much I could cut. We had a bare-bones budget. And then it hit me—we didn't have an expense issue; we had an income issue. It was the same conclusion you came to."

The diner's cook placed the bacon on the stove. They could hear the soft sizzle.

"Again, like you, I realized I had to make more money," said Cary.

"You must have been stressed, too," replied Austin.

"You would think, but no, not really," contemplated Cary. "You see, Marilyn and I had a deep trust in God. We knew he could provide us whatever he wanted."

"So you just waited for a check to show up in the mail?" questioned Austin, half joking.

Cary smiled. "No. Of course not. Trusting in God doesn't mean we don't do anything. He could have done that, but I knew that sometimes God provides checks and other times he provides us opportunities to make checks. So I decided to pray, work hard, and trust God with the results."

Cary brought his coffee cup up to his mouth but stopped before taking a drink. "Of course, you already know this stuff. You're a pastor."

Austin nodded with his lips pressed tightly together. He did know this—his brain knew it. But this morning his brain needed to remind his heart.

"Work hard and trust God," Austin voiced, somewhat to Cary but mostly to himself.

The problem was, it didn't matter how hard he worked for the church, they couldn't increase his pay. "But the church can't pay me more."

"And neither could the hardware store," replied Cary. "They didn't have any extra hours to give me."

"Here you go, guys." The waitress placed their plates on the table.

"I'll tell you what, you and Brooklyn meet me at the Hodges's house this evening at 6:00 pm. We're going to sell some lemonade."

Cary smiled and pulled out a pen from his pocket and wrote down an address on a napkin. Cary then slid the napkin over to Austin. Austin looked at the napkin. Under the address it read, "Work hard. Trust God."

"Will you meet me here?" asked Cary, pointing to the address.

"Sure. We'll be there."

Cary smiled again. "Great. Let's eat."

Meant for More

I have a friend who is a successful businessman. In fact, he was so successful he no longer needed to work to support himself, his wife, and their child. He had made enough money selling his business that he could spend his days walking up and down the beach in front of his condominium.

And that's exactly what he did.

For about two weeks.

After two weeks of beach walking, he grew restless. Something wasn't right. He was living "the dream," but he wasn't satisfied. He began to realize that the life he was living was not what God had designed him for. God had given him passion, skills, and a desire to use them for something significant.

"I kept thinking, *This can't be it,*" he told me as he recalled the thoughts that used to bombard his mind.

He knew he was meant for more. So he went after more.

My friend traded in his stagnant, beach-walking life for one of action and creation. He started a new business and dove headfirst into serving his church. And he is one of the most financially successful, generous, and servant-hearted men I know.

Even as I write this, he is running a successful business for God's glory and the advancement of his kingdom.

He was designed for work.

And so are you.

Work—God's Good Idea (Seriously)

Work was God's idea, his good and perfect idea. I know, Monday morning doesn't always feel like God's good and perfect idea. But it was. It is.

Work was a pre-fall idea. When everything was good, before sin, there was work: "The LORD God took the man and placed him in the garden of Eden to work it and watch over it" (Gen. 2:15). He provided humans the world in its raw form and said, "Go to work. Use your talents and skills. Do something with this."

So, prior to sin entering the world, Adam and Eve worked and God provided. Work, like every other part of creation, was designed to bring God glory.

God is a generous God, and we are designed to reflect His generosity. But God is also a working God. He is not sedentary. He is active. Being created in His image, we are designed to reflect this as well. Work was designed for us, and we were designed for work.

When Adam and Eve sinned, when the fruit was eaten, work became more difficult. Toiling, strife, stress, and disappointment entered work. Like us, work became corroded by sin.

And then Monday mornings happened.

Then unnecessarily long meetings happened.

Then cubicles happened.

Then coworkers leaving their used K-Cups in the office Keurig machine happened.

This doesn't mean that all things related to work are bad, just like all things related to money aren't bad. We're still created for work, and it is created for us. Our work can still point to God's glory, reflecting who he is. And we can actually enjoy the work for which he has designed us.

Studies[1] have shown that those who work tend to experience greater levels of happiness than those who don't work. Those who work also tend to be healthier, both mentally and physically, than those who do not work. It is even suggested that those who continue working past traditional retirement years will experience greater mental and physical vigor than their peers who stop working, depending on the type of work.[2]

What do studies like these do?

These studies point back to God's design for us; we are meant to work, to use our talents and abilities for his glory. Work, when everything is as it should be, brings us satisfaction and even happiness.

Work is how we provide for ourselves and those who rely on us.

God's Work and Our Work

The Bible tells us that we are to work for our provisions—our food, clothes, housing, cars.

Adam and Eve worked for their provisions. They cared for the garden. Jesus worked for his provisions. He was a carpenter. Paul worked for his provisions. He was a tentmaker. Timothy worked for his provisions. He was a pastor.

The book of Proverbs shows us that the way to provide for ourselves and our family is work.

> "The one who works his land will have plenty of food, but whoever chases fantasies lacks sense." (Prov. 12:11)

> "The slacker craves, yet has nothing, but the diligent is fully satisfied." (Prov. 13:4)

> "There is profit in all hard work, but endless talk leads only to poverty." (Prov. 14:23)

We work to provide. We play an important role in having our needs and the needs of others met.

At the same time the Bible tells us that God is the one who richly provides us with all things to enjoy. He owns it all and can provide it all.

He tells us not to worry about the future (Matt. 6:25) or even presume upon the future (James 4:13–16). We are to trust in God's provision.

This tension of God's designing and calling us to work for our provision and at the same time trusting in him to provide has created some problems on how we view making money. We usually find ourselves relating to one of four types of people—Hardworking Heathens, Driven Disciples, Undevout Dropouts, or Slow-Moving Saints.

(Please don't take the labels too seriously.)

Each of these groups has some Go-Getter (relying on self for provisions) and some Surrender (relying on God for provisions) in them. But their mix of each varies, creating different outcomes.

THE GO-GETTER/SURRENDER MATRIX

GO-GETTER	Hardworking Heathens	Driven Disciples
	Undevout Dropouts	Slow-Moving Saints

SURRENDER

Let's take a quick look at these four types of people:

Undevout Dropouts

Undevout Dropouts go light on the Go-Getter and Surrender.

These people pretty much never get in the game. They simply don't care. They don't put in much effort, but they are also not assuming God will simply provide whatever they need. Instead, they just don't care. They are not living by faith; they are living by laziness and are completely fine with its results.

Hardworking Heathens

Hardworking Heathens are heavy on the Go-Getter and light on the Surrender.

The Hardworking Heathen lives by Hezekiah 2:19: "God helps those who help themselves." Before you nod your head in agreement, that's not a real verse. And Hezekiah is not an actual book in the Bible. But it is essentially how the Hardworking Heathen views making money. It is all on them.

For the Hardworking Heathen, success is simply a consequence of his or her efforts. They are self-reliant to a fault. If the results do not turn out like they hoped, they blame themselves and vow to work harder. Hardworking Heathens are often stressed-out workaholics because they've placed the burden on themselves.

Jesus said, "Come to me, all of you who are weary and burdened, and I will give you rest" (Matt. 11:28). Hardworking Heathens experience no rest because they have not come to him.

Peter said to cast "all your cares on him, because he cares about you" (1 Pet. 5:7). Hardworking Heathens experience stress because they do not place their concerns on him.

They decide to use their own strength.

Slow-Moving Saints

Slow-Moving Saints are light on the Go-Getter and heavy on the Surrender.

God is in control of everything. And it is ultimately God who provides us anything we possess, including the money in our bank accounts. Slow-Moving Saints wholeheartedly believe this, which is good.

Unfortunately, they use the fact that God is in control over everything as a reason to avoid hard work or difficult decision-making. Instead of working hard or making tough decisions, they just say, "God will provide" and do little, if anything at all, to change their circumstances.

Proverbs 6:6–11 warns against laziness:

> Go to the ant, you slacker! Observe its ways and become wise. Without leader, administrator, or ruler, it prepares its provisions in summer; it gathers its food during harvest. How long will you stay in bed, you slacker? When will you get up from your sleep? A little sleep, a little slumber, a little folding of the arms to rest, and your poverty will come like a robber, your need, like a bandit.

Tell us how you *really* feel about it, Solomon.

Slow-Moving Saints assume that when something is difficult, like making more money, it must not be God's will for their lives. They act as if everything provided by God must come easy. They just want to wake up, walk out the door, eat their manna, and then go back in their house.

And, not surprisingly, their inaction results in lack of change in their circumstances.

Driven Disciples

Driven Disciples have a good mix of Go-Getter and Surrender in them.

They say yes to hard work and yes to God's control over everything.

They understand that God has called them to work, which can be difficult, and that their effort matters. They don't view themselves as a helpless leaf, being carried by the wind, powerless over their current circumstances. They reason that since Jesus had to work for his provision while on earth, they should expect no less.

Driven Disciples believe their decisions and actions make a difference.

At the same time, they know God is the Provider. He is in control, which does not push them to laziness but to trust and peace.

They are not like the Slow-Moving Saints—they work hard. But they are not stressed like the Hardworking Heathens. They are comforted to know that, while they work hard, the results of that work are under God's control. They work hard, do the best they can, and trust God.

> **Driven Disciples believe their decisions and actions make a difference. At the same time, they know God is the Provider.**

You can probably guess which one we should strive to be.

God is in control of everything. He is the one who richly provides us with all things to enjoy. Trust in God and experience the peace he offers, even during difficult financial circumstances.

But don't use this as an excuse to avoid work. God has designed you to work.

Your actions make a difference.

Your decisions make a difference.

Your effort makes a difference.

Your work can and will make a difference.

Be a Go-Getter.

Be under complete surrender to God and trust in his provision.

Be a Driven Disciple. Work hard and find peace, knowing God is in control.

Question to consider: Where do I find myself on the Go-Getter/Surrender Matrix?

The Making Money Taboo

I don't have a problem discussing money. I know, shocking. And one of the main reasons I am comfortable with the topic is how I view money, which was in step 1 of your Find More Money Workflow.

For many Christians, money is a taboo topic. You shouldn't talk about it. And you really shouldn't talk about *making* money—that topic is super taboo. But why? Why, when the Bible says so much about money, do we say so little?

The Prevalence of Greed

Examples of individuals pursuing more money for the wrong reasons are everywhere. Their motivation is building their kingdom, not God's kingdom. They are tightfisted instead of openhanded. Christians do not want to be perceived in that way, so we run from the topic.

We See Others with Less

We experience a sense of guilt. While we talk and think about making more money, we are aware that there are those who have far greater needs than we have in our community and around the world. And so we feel guilty about pursuing more money.

We Have Critics in Our Lives

Most of us have people in our lives who we know would criticize our attempt at making more money. They will say that making more money should not be the concern of a Christian. They know just enough Bible to be a critic but not enough Bible to fully understand God's perspective on money.

We Know Our Own Hearts

If we are honest, most of us are keenly aware of the allure money presents. We understand why Jesus spoke so frequently on the topic. The temptation is there for us to chase money for the sake of having more money, to place our hope in money. So we flee from it.

There are reasons making money is a taboo topic. But should it be? Does a right understanding of God's design for us and money cause us to flee the topic or run toward it and engage it? Let me provide you the following points to consider.

God is not opposed to wealth. He is opposed to hoarding wealth. There is a difference. This does not mean everyone is or should be wealthy. The master in the parable of the talents dispensed different amounts of resources to each servant. So it is with us. God provides much to some and little to others. He provides some with the ability to make money and build wealth, like my friend at the beginning of this chapter. And this is okay. It's not about the amount but the stewardship of it. And God ultimately provides it all.

Remember, working for our provision was also God's idea. Work was God's idea from the beginning. The Bible tells us that working for our provision is a good thing.

Remember, God designed us for generosity. God provides us resources to enjoy and advance his kingdom. Again, it is not wrong to have wealth. It is wrong to hoard wealth.

Financial health is a means to living and giving generously (and sometimes it takes making money to get us there). And this is where you are, wanting to live out God's design for you and your money but with an obstacle in your path. And increasing your income may be a way to overcome that obstacle.

The world pretty much has a monopoly on the money conversation. Because of this, we believe there is only one motivation behind making money—greed. We don't talk about other biblical possibilities, which only perpetuates the idea that money and making money are evil. We don't learn about money, which leads us to be poor managers of it, which stifles our ability to use it for God's mission.

It's as if Satan saw how often God talks about money, how important it is to him, and found a way to ensure that the message would not get out. He saw the potential Great Commission impact, and he found a way to shut down the conversation. He made God's teachings taboo.

This bothers me. And it should bother you. Don't hide this book from your friends. Don't run from the making money conversation. You have a mission. We all do. And sometimes making more money is exactly what you need to do.

God and Side Gigs

"God provided a job."

I've heard this statement made many times. You probably have as well. Often it is the result of much prayer and hard work. A job was desperately needed. So they prayed for a job. They worked hard to get a job.

And then, "God provided a job."

It is a statement that celebrates God's goodness as Provider, God working through the efforts of an individual.

We all experience difficulties in life, and some of those difficulties lie in the area of finances. Some are self-inflicted—too much debt was accumulated. But others are not—the line of work just doesn't pay that much.

Regardless, you need additional income.

I don't want to presume on God. But I also don't want you to overlook the possibility that God's provision may come in the form of a side gig.

Through prayer and hard work, God can and does provide jobs.

Likewise, through prayer and hard work, God can and does provide side gigs. God is no less at work in providing jobs than he is in providing side gigs. God is the Provider, and sometimes his provision comes in the form of side income through gigs.

I know many who have seen this to be true.

Look, you have a money problem. But you also have a potential money solution.

God has put you in a time and place where making additional income is easier than ever.

So rely on God—cast all your cares on him. And work hard.

And maybe, at the end of this journey, with margin finally in your finances, you will be able to say, "God provided a side gig."

Find more money.
Get financially healthy.
Advance God's kingdom among the broken.

STEP 3

Know Your *Find More Money* Goal

Austin's mouth was only able to form one word when he saw the house: *Whoa.*

"Are you sure this is the right place?" questioned Brooklyn.

"It has to be. There's Cary's truck."

Austin drove their car down the long, oak-lined driveway. The house was huge.

"I'm pretty sure this is referred to as a chateau," commented Brooklyn.

They pulled up next to Cary's truck. Cary and Sophia were in it. When they saw Austin and Brooklyn, they stepped out. Austin and Brooklyn got out of their car as well.

"Glad you could join me!" exclaimed Cary.

"Nice place," remarked Austin.

Cary went to the back of his truck. He pulled out a sledgehammer and handed it to Austin. He then pulled out a chain saw and gave it to Brooklyn.

"All right!" grinned Cary. "Let's get to work!"

"Uh, I'm not sure whatever type of work you want me to do is appropriate for a pregnant woman," Brooklyn said hesitantly.

Austin looked over at Sophia. She was giggling really hard.

"I'm just joking!" said Cary. He took back the sledgehammer and chain saw.

After he put the tools back in the truck, Cary continued. "You need more money. Well, I'm going to show you how I made more money during tight times for Marilyn and me. And I'll let you make some money as well."

Austin and Brooklyn liked the sound of that.

"So, how much money do you need?" asked Cary.

Austin was slightly caught off guard by the question. "What do you mean?"

"Well, you need a goal. How else will you know when you've accomplished what you need to accomplish? Here is how I determined what I needed to make."

Cary pulled out a piece of paper and showed it to Austin and Brooklyn. On it were the words:

Money Milestones

Milestone 1: Start giving.

Milestone 2: Save $1,500 for a minor emergency.

Milestone 3: Max out your 401(k) or 403(b) match.

Milestone 4: Pay off all debt except your mortgage.

Milestone 5: Save 3–6 months of living expenses for a job-loss level emergency.

Milestone 6: Put 15 percent of your gross income to retirement.

Milestone 7: Save for college or pay off your mortgage.

Milestone 8: Live generously.

"I'm on Milestone 7," Cary said proudly.

"Wow. Congrats. Do you always keep this on you?" asked Austin.

"No. I have a copy at home. I just brought this for you."

Cary handed the paper to Austin. As Austin held it, Brooklyn leaned over to look at it.

"I like that giving is first," noted Brooklyn. "It follows what we find in the Bible."

"Just like my capsules at home: Give—Save—Live!" said Sophia.

"Capsules?" questioned Brooklyn.

"They're jars," explained Cary. "They help her follow God's plan for money."

"Oh, neat," replied Brooklyn.

Austin thought for a moment. "I guess we need to go after Milestone 2a."

"2a?" questioned Cary.

"2a," confirmed Austin. "We have a known financial emergency coming up. And we don't need $1,500 to cover it. We need $7,500. We need $1,500 per month."

Sophia pulled out a notebook and began writing.

Cary noticed the young couple looking at Sophia. "She always takes notes."

"Impressive," said Brooklyn.

Cary looked at the house. "Well, maybe this evening can help. Let's go build a deck."

Austin and Brooklyn looked at each other. This was not what they expected.

————

You Need a Goal

Before taking a side gig, one of the most important questions to answer is this: *How much money do I need?*

This seemingly simple question often gets lost on a side gigger's journey to finding more money. For those who don't necessarily need additional income—the hobbyists—knowing this answer is not always necessary. But for you, the one who really needs to increase your income, answering this question is essential.

Imagine you and your family decide to go on a vacation. You really feel like your family needs it. Over the past few months, busy schedules have resulted in significant stress. Your family needs a break.

So you pack up the car and turn on the ignition. There is just one, small problem—you don't know your destination. You don't know where you're going. You don't know whether you should back out of your house's driveway and go left or right.

Sure, that's an unlikely scenario—at least, I hope it is. But imagine the reaction of your family. Did you just alleviate stress? Are things better now for your family, sitting in the car, realizing you have no idea where you are going? Probably not. In fact, your attempt at vacationing has just made everything worse. Even if you get on the road, the family is still wondering where, when, and how. And so are you. You now have more questions and stress than when you started.

WITHOUT A GOAL   WITH A GOAL

START ?   START———→ FINISH

Goals matter. They matter for your vacation, and they matter for your finances.

Right now you have good intentions. You are motivated to increase your income. But without goals good intentions quickly dissipate.

Goals identify your destination.

Goals help you plan.

Goals allow you to see success. You are able to see not just how far you need to go but also how far you've come.

Goals can also bring people together. They unite. If you are married, your spouse will be more understanding of the sacrifices taken to increase your income because he or she knows the goal.

The 8 Money Milestones

Before identifying your specific money goal, let's look at the 8 Money Milestones. I first introduced The Money Milestones in *The Money Challenge.*[1] They provide a map for obtaining financial health for the sake of giving and living generously. I love hearing success stories from those who follow the milestones, stories from people like Noah in Texas who paid off more than $50,000 in debt on his journey to living the generous, kingdom-advancing life.

I hope you are the next success story.

As you read the milestones, consider where you are on the journey.

Milestone I: Start giving.

Generosity is the foundation upon which real, biblical financial health is founded. According to the Bible, generosity is our priority. We are to give our first and our best. Wherever you find yourself financially, financial health starts with giving.

Milestone 2: Save $1,500 for a minor emergency.

You will get hit with a financial emergency. Encouraging, right? Your dishwasher will break. A tire will go flat. When these minor emergencies happen, many resort to credit cards, perpetuating their financial challenges. Be different from everyone else. Set aside money so you can cover the emergency with cash.

Milestone 3: Max out your 401(k) or 403(b) match.

If a company match is available to you, get it. It's part of your employee benefits package. Ignoring the match is ignoring your money. The long-term financial impact of maxing out your match is tremendous. Don't miss out on it.

Milestone 4: Pay off all debt except your mortgage.

To pay off debt, I recommend a well-known method called the Snowball Method. This method encourages you to pay off debts from the smallest balance to the largest balance. Once a debt is paid off, you apply the amount you were paying to the smaller debt to the larger debt. Like a snowball rolling down a hill, the amount you are able to put toward debt gradually increases.

Milestone 5: Save three to six months of living expenses for a job-loss level emergency.

If you are single and without children, lean toward the three-month end of the spectrum. If you are married with children, lean toward the six-month end of the spectrum. Let those for whom you are financially responsible help determine how much you need saved.

Milestone 6: Put 15 percent of your gross income to retirement.

Plan on making your retirement years the most generous, openhanded years of your life. Set aside money for retirement so you are not a financial burden on others and can have even more time and money to put toward advancing God's kingdom.

Milestone 7: Save for college or pay off your mortgage.

Too many assume mortgage payments are just like utility bills, payments that will be with them for the rest of their lives. Believe it or not, you don't always have to have a mortgage payment. You can be mortgage free. Sure, it takes time and intentionality, but it is worth it. Imagine what life would look like without a mortgage payment. Imagine what your generosity would look like without a mortgage payment. Imagine what your retirement would look like without a mortgage payment.

If you have kids, consider initially focusing on college instead of your mortgage. More than likely, college expenses will be a more immediate issue.

Milestone 8: Live generously.

You have financial health. But not so you can spend money on whatever you want. You have financial health so you can give and live ridiculously generous lives, being a part of God's mission in a way you never imagined.

Those are your 8 Money Milestones. Get to know them. Maybe put them up somewhere in your house to encourage your journey.

Using these Money Milestones, let's consider how much more money you need.

Your *Find More Money* Goal

As you read through each of the milestones, you probably found yourself gauging where you stand in relation to the milestones.

Maybe you realized that generosity hasn't been a part of your finances. According to the Bible, this is the priority for our finances.

Maybe you realized you had yet to set aside money for a minor emergency. The good news is that this step is usually one of the quickest milestones for people to achieve.

Maybe you need to get rid of debt. Debt kills a person's ability to give and save.

Maybe you need to set aside three to six months' worth of living expenses to guard against a major financial emergency.

Maybe you have yet to seriously save for retirement, and 15 percent of your gross income seems a long way off.

Maybe you are concerned about your children's college expenses.

Maybe you want to get rid of your mortgage.

You need to identify two goals—your *Money Milestone* goal and your *Find More Money* goal. Both are monthly goals. Sometimes these goals are the same number, but they often differ. The *Money Milestone* goal feeds into the *Find More Money* goal.

Let me help you determine both.

Find the Gap, Create a Budget

It's time to do an investigation on your finances. We're looking for the financial gap. This gap is the difference between how much money you need each month compared to how much money you make each month. Knowing this gap will help you identify your goals, your destination.

And the best ways to see your gap is to create a monthly budget. Here's how to do it:

Step 1: Determine Your Monthly Milestone Goal

What are your financial goals? I want you to think beyond just paying the bills. That should be a given. When considering your goals, use the 8 Money Milestones as a guide. How much money per month do you need to achieve your next Milestone? This is your Monthly Milestone Goal.

Do you want to give more? Do you want to set aside $500 per month, reaching for your emergency savings goal? Do you want to have $1,000 going toward debts, crushing them quickly? Or retirement?

Just pick one Milestone Goal. If you find yourself desiring to hit multiple goals, refer to the 8 Money Milestones, and pick whatever takes place first. Once you hit your most pressing milestone, you can then move to the next.

First, write down the next Money Milestone you need to hit:

My Next Money Milestone: _____

Next, write down your Monthly Milestone Goal.

Monthly Money Milestone Goal: _____

Step 2: Determine your typical monthly income.

For many this is pretty simple—you look at your paycheck. You have a regular salary, and this is revealed on your monthly or bimonthly paychecks. For some, each paycheck varies—maybe because you are a commission-based employee. For others different seasons provide different income—maybe you are a teacher. If this is you, average your monthly paychecks. Or if some months have higher income than others, adjust the budget accordingly.

Be sure to use net (after-tax) income. This is probably the amount that hits your bank account.

Write your monthly income here.

Monthly Income: _____

Step 3: Determine your typical monthly expenditures.

Go back and look at your past three month's expenses. All of them—grocery, medical, utility, entertainment, etc. Try to group expenses into categories. You don't want to go crazy with the categories. Keep it manageable. Then, by looking at the past three months, find the average expenditures for each category.

If you receive pretax (gross) income, be sure to include your taxes.

Now add it all up. This is how much, on average, you spend each month.

Write down your total monthly expenditures here:

Monthly Expenditures: _____

Step 4: Adjust your expenditures to fit your income (and your ability to give and save).

Fair warning—this will be the frustrating part for you. Figure out how you can fit your expenditures into your income by reducing or eliminating—how you can live within your means.

And this is what will make it extra frustrating—you probably aren't able to, even when reductions or eliminations are made.

If you were able to make any adjustments in your expenditures, write down your adjusted monthly expenditures here. If adjustments are not possible, use your prior Monthly Expenditures number.

Adjusted Monthly Expenditures: _____

Now I am going to ask you to do something even more frustrating—look at the monthly goal you identified. Put it in your budget as well. Again, I want your *Find More Money* goal to move you beyond just getting your bills paid.

That gap between your monthly income and your expenditures plus your monthly goal is your Monthly *Find More Money* goal. To put it into a formula:

(Adjusted Monthly Expenditures + Monthly Milestone Goal) – Monthly Income = Monthly Find More Money Goal

Using the formula above, fill out your own formula:

(_____ + _____)
        - _____ =
_____

Knowing your Monthly *Find More Money* goal will provide greater clarity as you move forward. You will have a better handle on your finances and be equipped to make planning decisions that are not based on a whim or a feeling. Knowing your goal will help you find more money.

Now on to step 4 in your *Find More Money Workflow*—Know You.

Find more money.
Get financially healthy.
Advance God's kingdom among the
marginalized.

STEP 4

Know You

After two hours of sawing and hammering, they were done. The deck wasn't complete. There was still more work to do. But it had grown dark.

Outside the house Cary pulled out a $100 bill and handed it to Austin.

"Here you go," said Cary.

"Twenty-five dollars per hour for both of us?" questioned Austin. "That seems a little high."

"Yeah, I'm pretty sure my work wasn't that beneficial to the project," chuckled Brooklyn. "This may surprise you, but it was my first time building a deck."

Cary laughed. "I may or may not have been able to tell. But I'm happy to pay you both for the work."

Sophia opened her notebook again. "Now you have $7,400 left!"

"And I am still impressed," commented Brooklyn.

Sophia just smiled back.

"Man, if you would pay us $100 every night, we would have more than enough for the delivery," said Austin with a grin.

Cary smiled back. "I don't know if I can pay you $100 every night, but I can introduce you to the world of side gigs."

"Side gigs?" questioned Brooklyn.

"Yes," nodded Cary. "Making money outside of your primary job. It's how I managed to get through a financially difficult time in my life."

Cary read Austin and Brooklyn's faces. They were skeptical.

"I mentioned it to Austin this morning. A few years ago Marilyn and I found ourselves unable to pay our bills, much like you. But here's what I didn't tell Austin: One day I was at the hardware store, helping a customer figure out a small plumbing issue. In the midst of our conversation, she asked me if she could just pay me to do the work. I needed the money, so I did it after my shift."

Cary paused.

"After I did the work, I had a thought: *What if I could keep my job and do handyman work on the side?* I started researching the possibility and realized a lot of people out there, just like me, earn income outside their primary jobs."

"And you're still doing side gigs," noted Brooklyn.

"I want to knock out Milestone 7—paying off my mortgage and having money for Sophia's college."

"I think she might get a scholarship," said Brooklyn, smiling at Sophia.

Austin quickly interjected, "What if Brooklyn and I started doing handyman work?" He turned to Brooklyn. "We could be like Chip and Joanna Gaines, except we do handyman work!"

Brooklyn's straight face revealed that she was less than enthusiastic about the idea. "That sounds miserable to me. Did you see my work today? I mean, if it's what we have to do, I'm up for it, but I would much rather do something else. Sorry to crush your dream, Austin."

Cary understood. "Look, I've met many people with side gigs. The side gigs that work out best tend to be found at the intersection of these three questions: *What am I passionate about? What am I good at? And what will people pay me to do?*"

Austin pressed his index finger against his lips as he pondered. "I don't know; handyman work actually works for all three of those questions. I love connecting with people. I'm pretty good with home repairs. And people will pay for that type of work. At least, they have in the past."

Brooklyn shook her head in disagreement. "No. No. And no. I don't like it. I am not good at it. And no one will pay me to do it."

Cary chuckled. "Guys, you don't have to do the same thing! Brooklyn, you can find a different side gig that works for you. Just take some time and consider what you're passionate about, what you're good at, and what people will pay you to do. Go home and think about it."

"Our goal is $1,500 per month," Austin thought out loud. "We need side gigs where we can at least make $1,500 per month." He turned to Cary, "Hey, do you have anybody that may need some help with home repairs?"

Cary looked up at the now-night sky. "You know, I just might."

––––––––––

Your Trifecta

A friend of mine, Kristin, is a native Floridian. What most do once or twice as kids, she did all the time—go to Walt Disney

World. She loved Disney, even as she became a parent of her own kids. It was part of her childhood and now part of her children's.

Kristin was and is a Disney aficionado, so she decided to make additional income off of her passion and expertise. Kristin connected with Travelmation, an authorized Disney vacation planning service provider. She's now sharing her passion and expertise with future Walt Disney World guests, crafting incredible Disney experiences. And, of course, she makes money doing it.

Psalm 139:13–14 says, "For it was you who created my inward parts; you knit me together in my mother's womb. I will praise you because I have been remarkably and wondrously made."

God made each one of us with a unique combination of looks and likes. No one is just like me, and no one is just like you. To ignore this truth would be unwise, especially as you consider which side gig you should take.

So which gig is your gig? In an ideal world it is the place where God-given passion and skill collide with a real opportunity to increase your income. Passion, skill, and opportunity—these are your trifecta. This is the point where you will find not only money but also motivation to endure through the inevitable challenges.

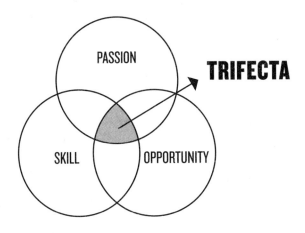

Let's take a look at these three parts.

Passion (What Do I Love?)

I frequently tell my boys that God created them uniquely, that there is no one else exactly like them. One of the reasons I do this is because I have noticed, as most parents do, that it's true. Each of my kids has different likes. One is into music, one is into sports, and the other, right now, is into keeping his parents up at night. And I want them to chase those things (except for the one keeping his parents up at night—I'm hoping he finds a more constructive passion).

The same is true for you. We have an unfathomably creative God. Everyone he creates is unique. There is no one else—past, present, or future—who is exactly like you. You have your own likes, your own passions.

At least, you did.

As adults we sometimes find ourselves in survival mode, setting aside passions for, well, just getting by. We don't have time for our passions. The finiteness of time seems to squeeze them out of us. And after a while, we forget that we once had passions, dreams.

As a starting point for finding your gig, I want you to remember the passions you once had. If you are going to make money outside your day-to-day job, doing something that excites you is ideal. So, if you forgot what your passions once were, let me help you rediscover them by asking a few questions.

Passion Question I: What Did You like to Do as a Kid?

Before the pressures of adulthood squeezed out your passions, what did you dream about doing? As a teenager I sat in my room and came up with business ideas. I read business books.

Seriously.

You can call me weird; it's fine.

But what about you? What were your passions as a kid? What did you love?

Put your answers here: _____

Passion Question 2: What Do You Hate to Stop Doing?

When do you find yourself thinking, *Ugh. I really don't want to quit now. I wish I had more time?*

What projects, even while you are not doing them, do you find yourself still thinking about? What are you doing when time seems to fly by? If you hate to stop doing something, you may have found a passion.

Put your answers here: _____

Passion Question 3: What Bothers You?

It bothered me how past financial decisions were crippling individuals' ability to live generously. So I wrote a book, *The Money Challenge.*

I was bothered that money was regularly referred to as a divider in marriages when it can actually be a great unifier. So I wrote another book, *The Marriage Challenge.*[1]

And I was bothered that most Christian personal finance books deal with only one side of the financial equation. So, I'm writing this book.

What bothers you? What's bothering you is pointing you toward your passion.

Put your answers here: _____

Passion Question 4: What Do You Love to Learn and Talk About?

I sometimes give a warning before I dive into the topic of personal finances—"You may be here for a while."

When you are passionate about something, you can't help but talk about it. You get excited. Your eyes light up.

When you can learn more about the topic, you go for it. You read the books, watch the videos, or even take the classes. You've searched for it so many times on the Internet, Google Search automatically provides results without your needing to type a word. Okay, that doesn't actually happen—yet—but you get the point.

Whatever you can't stop talking and learning about could be your passion. So, what do you love to learn and talk about?

Put your answers here: _____

Hold on to your passion answers. We'll use them at the end of this chapter.

Skill (What Am I Good At?)

When finding more money, you need to consider what you are actually good at doing, right this moment. This doesn't mean you should not aspire to gain new skills or improve skills that aren't your best. But you need money. Therefore, you must focus on what is already available to you.

In middle school I used to think I had a pretty good shot at playing college basketball. I thought that averaging 2.5 points per game meant I had the skills needed to play at the next level. Professional basketball was a stretch, but college basketball was within reach.

Remembering those days makes me laugh.

Sometimes we think our skills are better than they really are. In order to determine the skills you will use to increase your income, lay aside your opinion and consider the opinions of others. Here are a few questions to help you identify your skills.

Skills Question I: What Do You Currently Do at Work?

Here's why I start with this question—someone is already paying you to use certain skills. They have found value in a certain skill set you possess. In fact, they find it so valuable, they are willing to pay you for it.

What type of skills do you use at work?

Administrative skills?

Writing and editing skills?

Teaching skills?

Carpentry skills?

Design skills?

Mechanical skills?

You use certain skills at work. Write those down, and let them be a starting point as you dive into the next two questions.

Put your answers here: _____

Skills Question 2: What Do Others Say You Are Good At?

It's often said that we shouldn't care what others think. And sometimes we shouldn't. But in this case you should care.

This is going to sound harsh: it doesn't matter what you think you're good at. You don't choose someone to paint your house because the painter thinks he is good at painting. You choose someone to paint your house because you think he is good at painting.

Take some time and consider what others have said you are good at.

At work, what skills did your supervisor or those around you praise? For what abilities have others applauded you?

If you can't recall a time when someone has commented on your skills and abilities, ask someone. Ask, "What do you think I am best at?" or "What do you think are my top three skills?" Ask your friends. Ask your coworkers. Ask your supervisor. Get to know where others think you excel.

What do others say you are good at?

Put your answers here: _____

Skills Question 3: When Do People Ask for Your Help?

You know what people don't ask me to do? Rap. I have yet to receive a single request for my rapping abilities. I regularly receive requests for help regarding personal finances, but no rapping requests. If someone is looking for a rapper, they don't send me a text, email, or tweet. I am nowhere on their radar.

There's a simple reason for the lack of requests—I don't have the skills to do it well.

One of the best ways to identify skills others find valuable is by considering what others ask you to do.

When do people ask you for help?

Put your answers here: _____

Opportunity (What Will Someone Pay Me to Do?)

You can be passionate about writing. You may even have incredible writing skills. But, in order to find more money, you must have the opportunity, where someone will actually pay you for what you do.

If you only have passion, you have the makings of a dream. If you have passion and skills, you have the makings of a hobby. In order to turn passion and skills into money, you must find the opportunity.

And you will either need to be an *opportunity maker* or an *opportunity taker*.

I. Opportunity Makers

Opportunity makers are entrepreneurs. You start a profitable business. Now, this does not mean you create a $500 million company. You may create a business that makes a $1,000 profit each month.

The key word with this route is *profit*. Revenue (the money you make) minus expenses (the money you spend) equals profit. After covering your expenses, money must be left over. Otherwise, you are adding to, not helping, your money problem.

Here are the plusses and minuses for opportunity makers.

+	−
Ability to express creativity	More administrative work
Total control	Responsible for making profit
You keep all profit	Can take time to make money
No ceiling on income growth	No guarantees

2. Opportunity Takers

Opportunity takers partner with existing businesses.

If you need money now or have no money to put toward the creation of a business, you should consider being an opportunity taker.

Many, if not most, turn to this option. Instead of going into business for themselves, they find contract work with another business. They offer their services to a business or person who has a need for them. My friend Kristin is an example of this. She makes money by helping Travelmation succeed.

Those who earn money by partnering with companies like Uber or Lyft are opportunity takers.

Consider the positives and negatives for the opportunity-taker route.

+	**–**
Make money quickly	Limits creativity
Less administrative work	Limited control
Lower stress	Ceiling on income

What are you? Are you an opportunity maker or an opportunity taker? What fits your personality and your current financial need? Do you need money now? Or are you willing to wait, comfortable with the higher risk, higher reward option of starting your own side-gig business?

Put your answer here: _____

Get Your Priorities Ready

Follow your passion! Sure—as long as it pays. As I mentioned earlier, the ideal scenario is that you find a place where passion, skills, and opportunity intersect. And I hope you find that sweet spot.

But let's assume the sweet spot never materializes. Or you are in a place where you simply can't make it until the ideal scenario shows up. You need money now! What do you do? You prioritize the three.

Priority 1: Opportunity

If you find a legitimate gig that allows you to make side income, but you aren't necessarily passionate about the work, and maybe it doesn't quite fit your gifting, you can still take it. It's okay. In fact, if there are no other opportunities for additional income, you should take it if you have an immediate need for additional income. You can still search for a gig that aligns with your passion and skill, but go ahead and start solving your income problem now.

Priority 2: Skills

You might be able to find a side gig that doesn't necessarily fit your skill set, but it's better if it does, even if you are not passionate about the work. Work that aligns with your skill set will come easier to you, and your customer will be more satisfied because the work is completed at a high level. Which may result in repeated work requests or referrals.

Priority 3: Passion

Your last priority is your passion. Now, if you are not pressed to find more money, elevate passion in your hunt for outside income. However, when I talk to most people about needing more income, they don't have much time to waste. The bills need to get paid. Debt needs to get crushed. If this is you, don't completely write off finding work that matches your passion—just be realistic. You need to increase your income, and sometimes this means taking work that doesn't always generate a great deal of personal excitement.

My Hope for You

My friend, Mackenzie, is incredibly skilled at teaching children. And she loves doing it. It is a place where her passion and skills collide. She wanted to pursue her passion, use her skills, and make a little money doing it. Mackenzie was a new mom, and finances were tight for her family.

She began teaching part-time at a local preschool. But then she found a way to make even more money, while maintaining her teaching job. By doing a little research, Mackenzie found her opportunity. She now works for an organization that teaches English as a second language to children on the other side of the planet.

Seriously.

She teaches online via video and makes about $20 per hour doing it. Mackenzie knew her passion and skills and found the perfect side-gig opportunity. It was a trifecta.

I genuinely hope you find your ideal side gig. I hope you find a gig where passion, skill, and, of course, opportunity meet. But I also hope that if you are in a place of need, you won't run from good opportunities, even if they don't perfectly align with your passion and skill set.

Your gig is out there. You can find more money. In the next step we are going to look at a few gigs that may work for you.

Working Your *Find More Money* Workflow

1. Using the passion questions and answers, write down your top three recurring passions in the spaces below.

Passion 1: _____

Passion 2: _____

Passion 3: _____

2. Now, using the skills questions and answers, write down your top three recurring skills in the spaces below.

Skill 1: _____

Skill 2: _____

Skill 3: _____

You have your passions. You have your skills. In the next step you'll get several ideas to help you with the opportunity portion of the trifecta.

Find more money.
Get financially healthy.
Advance God's kingdom among the unreached.

STEP 5

Get a Gig

A ustin, we need money now!" Brooklyn said in a heated tone. "We don't have time for you to ramp up a handyman side gig!"

Austin and Brooklyn were back at their townhouse. Working with Cary provided a moment of hope. But only a moment. Austin wanted to dive headfirst into handyman work, but Brooklyn had legitimate concerns. Austin was starting from scratch. He had no clients. And no clients meant no money.

Financial stress seemed to be taking its toll on the young couple. With each passing day, they were getting closer to a financial disaster. And they felt it.

"Sure, there's risk," he agreed, "but the upside is, once I get things going, I can potentially make a lot more money than driving people around through a ride-sharing service. Cary did it."

"The key word you said was *potentially*," Brooklyn pointed out, still agitated. "And Cary worked at a hardware store. He was meeting people every day who had problems at their house."

Austin stopped himself from immediately replying. The words about to come out of his mouth would only make things worse. He sat down on the sofa and took a deep breath.

"Let's set aside my handyman idea for second," he calmly suggested. "Do you have thoughts about what you would like to do?"

"I do," Brooklyn replied. "I want to go shopping."

Austin's eyes looked to the left and then to the right. He furrowed his brow. "I don't think you fully understand our situation."

Brooklyn gave Austin a tight-lipped smile. "Not for me. I want to get paid to shop for someone else. I like shopping and it seems like a way to make some quick money."

She showed Austin a website. It was a grocery delivery service. "I did a quick Internet search on my phone while we were driving home. Someone puts in an order, then I go get the groceries and deliver them. I get paid for something I like to do." Brooklyn sat down next to Austin. "And I can start making money as soon as they approve me as a shopper, which is just a few days. What do you think?"

Austin nodded and thought for a second. "Okay, we need $1,500 per month for the next four months. What if you did the grocery delivery service and I tried doing handyman work?"

Brooklyn didn't seem completely on board. "Remember, I'm pregnant. I won't be able to work the full four months."

"Right. So, if we get to the end of the third month and are still struggling, I'll quit the handyman work and go shopping too."

Brooklyn laughed. "You are the most inefficient grocery shopper I have ever seen! You run all around the store looking for stuff. It takes you twice as long as it should."

Austin smiled back. He knew she was right. "Well, let's hope I don't have to be a shopper then."

"I would pay you *not* to shop for me," joked Brooklyn.

"Hey, that sounds like a good side-gig idea," said Austin, keeping the joke going. "Do you think it'll work?"

"Eh," replied Brooklyn, "I would stick to handyman work."

"You know, Jesus was a carpenter," said Austin. "So by me being a handyman . . ."

"Please don't go there."

"Yeah, I might be stretching it a little."

"Just a little," said Brooklyn.

Ordinary Side Giggers, like You

Chris Guillebeau has a great podcast called *Side Hustle School.* The concept of the podcast is pretty simple—he tells stories of individuals who found ways to make side income without quitting their day job.

He has found so many stories that he shares one per day. For the most part, they are all different gigs. It's pretty amazing. Even so, he is barely scratching the surface of stories about men and women making side income.

Let me share a few of my favorites stories he uncovered.

Max's Story[i]

Max had a hobby—fish, like the kind found in a fish tank. Over time he learned a lot about fish and the proper tanks for various kinds of fish.

Like many of us, Max had a full-time job that didn't provide much free time outside of work, but he wanted to share his knowledge of fish tanks. So he created a website: fishtankbank.com.

Pretty catchy, right? (Pun somewhat intended.)

On the site he reviews various fish tanks and links them back to Amazon, so a person could purchase the tank if they wanted.

He makes money if someone purchases the tank.

Amazon.com has what's called an affiliate program. This means they will pay someone who refers a purchaser to their site.

Over time people began going to Max's website, reading his reviews, and buying fish tanks. At the time of the recording, Max was earning $700 per month through the affiliate program.

Andrea's Story[2]

Andrea lived in Texas, loved dogs, and needed a way to make more money. She signed up as a pet sitter on Rover.com.

You may be familiar with Airbnb. Rover is like Airbnb but for dogs. Some who travel prefer that their dogs stay in someone's home instead of a kennel. They pay the pet sitter while they are out of town.

Andrea worked hard to become one of the most desirable pet sitters in her area and, at the time of the recording, makes up to $200 per day through Rover.com.

Andrew's Story[3]

Andrew is an industrial engineer. As you can imagine, he's a pretty handy guy. (I know, I'm stereotyping engineers.)

For fun, Andrew bought some slate and some equipment to carve the rock. His original plan was to carve out his last name and put it on the front of his house. Which he did. But in the process, he realized how easy it was to carve the rock.

For a subsequent project Andrew made a cutting board in the shape of his home state, Pennsylvania. He placed it on Etsy.com, a place where people can buy handcrafted goods, like Pennsylvania-shaped cutting boards.

And to his surprise someone bought it.

Andrew made more states and other products and listed them on Etsy as well. At the time of the recording, he had made $10,000 selling slate products.

Parker's Story[4]

Parker is an IT manager in Tennessee and needed some extra income to take care of his expenses. His job was incredibly consuming, so he didn't have much time to devote to extra work.

Since he had some IT know-how, he signed up on fiverr.com, a site that connects freelancers to those who need their services. Through an unexpected turn of events, he was asked to do a voice-over in English for a foreign company.

That company recommended him to another foreign company. And then it happened again.

And again.

And again.

At the time of the recording, Parker had made $8,000 doing English voice-overs for foreign companies.

Seriously.

Your Side Gig Is Out There

Entrepreneur magazine published a list of the top ten side gigs.[5]

1. Web and software development work (more than 625,000 freelancers)
2. Design and creative work (more than 600,000 freelancers)
3. Writing and translation work (more than 570,000 freelancers)
4. Administrative support work (more than 420,000 freelancers)
5. IT and networking work (more than 330,000 freelancers)
6. Customer service work (more than 230,000 freelancers)
7. Sales and marketing work (more than 180,000 freelancers)
8. Accounting and finance work (more than 165,000 freelancers)
9. Engineering and architecture work (more than 80,000 freelancers)
10. Data science work (more than 44,000 freelancers)

If you think none of these appeal to you, remember that opportunity is the most important part of your trifecta.

Second, you may be looking at the wrong part of the list. Don't focus on the gigs; focus on the people. Do you see the number of freelancers, real people, next to the gig? You should see that and think, *Certainly, if that many people can find a gig, I can too.*

The list should create a sense of hope and possibility.

There are a lot of opportunities out there.

I want to expose you to some of the opportunities real people, people like you, are finding in order to increase their income. My hope as you read these next few pages is for you to experience your aha moment.

You know your *why.* You know how much money you need to make. You have two parts of your trifecta—passions and skills.

In this chapter I hope you either find the missing piece to your trifecta or an opportunity idea suddenly hits you.

And then, aha, you realize that making additional income might actually happen, that your desire to tackle debt, save wisely, and live generously is within reach.

Traditional Part-Time Work

Now, some might not classify these as gigs, but I am going to include them anyway. You are already familiar with many traditional, part-time opportunities, and they should be in your arsenal of possible opportunities.

Part-Time Retail

Retail includes stores like Walmart, Target, Barnes and Noble, and Old Navy. These jobs tend not to pay a lot per hour, unless you are working during the holidays. According to Glassdoor. com,[6] the average pay for a part-time cashier at Walmart is $9 per hour. Assuming you work ten hours per week, this will add $390 of income per month.

Part-Time Food Service

Food-service gigs can range from serving tables to delivering pizzas to pouring lattes. These jobs often have hourly pay, but you make most of your money on tips. Ziprecruiter.com[7] reported that people who deliver pizzas average about $14 per hour, which provides you an additional $600 per month, working ten hours per week.

Other Part-Time Work

Part-time work extends well beyond retail and food service. I have a friend who worked with a landscaping company on weekends for additional income. You'll find a variety of traditional part-time opportunities out there.

The major drawback to these side gigs is lack of flexibility. This is why many in the side-gig economy don't pursue them. They need something where they have more control. Once again, you should not completely rule them out at this point; every opportunity needs to be on the table.

➕	➖
Predictable income	Limited income growth
Immediate income	Often "feels like a job"
Set schedule reduces procrastination	Limited flexibility and creativity

Gigs for Opportunity Takers

Some gigs are getting a lot of attention these days. In part this is due to the havoc they are wreaking on their respective industries. But it's also due to the number of people jumping into these gigs. The gigs you are about to see offer a ton of flexibility and tend not to be stressful unless driving stresses you out. You've probably heard of, or even used, some of these. They may be worth considering for your opportunity.

Drive People Around

I know, you already drive your kids around everywhere. But this is different. This time you get paid!

Two major players dominate what's known as ride sharing—Uber and Lyft. But the list is growing. Uber and Lyft drivers are essentially taking the place of taxis. The services are centered on a smartphone application (app). Customers request a driver, you pick them up and drive them to their destinations in your own car, and they pay you through the app.

To become a driver, you just need to download the Uber or Lyft app on your phone and apply to be a driver (they do have requirements for drivers). Once you're approved, you can start making money. According to Rideshareapp.com,[8] Lyft drivers make about $17.50 per hour, or $750 per month for ten hours per week. Many drivers are approved by both Uber and Lyft, which gives them more opportunities to drive.

Let People Drive Your Truck

Don't feel like driving people around? Just let them drive your car.

Fluid Truck Share (fluidtruck.com) connects people who need a truck (or car) to those who are willing to lend it out, for a fee of course. If you have a pickup truck, you've probably been asked several times if it can be used to move furniture (or other random items).

Now, you can make money saying yes.

Host People (or Pets)

Another gig you are probably familiar with is Airbnb (Airbnb. com). Airbnb is a web platform that connects people who need a place to stay with people who are willing to host someone for a fee. For guests, it's typically a budget-friendly alternative to hotels. Hosts earn additional income off your residence. Guests pay through the Airbnb platform. Airbnb takes a small cut of the rate and gives you the remaining amount. Income from Airbnb ranges dramatically. To determine how much money you can make, check out what others in your area are charging for comparable square footage, amenities, etc.

If you don't like people, host pets. In one of the prior stories, this is what Andrea did. There are several routes you can take with this. If you like pets and need to make some money, here are some companies to consider: Rover (rover.com), Wag! (wagwalking.com), and DogVacay (dogvacay.com).

Deliver Food

Food delivery services are becoming increasingly popular. There are two typical types of food delivery services—grocery and restaurant. Most services work in a similar manner. Food is picked up from the grocery store or restaurant and delivered to the customer. Your car will be needed for this.

Some of the more popular grocery delivery services include Shipt (shipt.com) and Instacart (instacart.com). Taking on a gig like this means you are both the shopper and the deliverer. The schedule is flexible. You let the company know what times you are available to work, and they try to connect you with a customer who needs groceries. Once a match has been made, you go to the grocery store, pick out the items on their list, and deliver the groceries to them.

To be considered a shopper, you will need to go to the company website and apply. According to Shipt.com,[9] shoppers make anywhere between $16 and $22 per hour. For ten hours of work per week, this can provide more than $700 per month—a great gig for those who like to shop.

Restaurant delivery services work in a similar way, but you don't shop. You just pick up the order from a restaurant and deliver it to the customer. If the customer orders a Crunchwrap Supreme from Taco Bell, you drive to Taco Bell, pick up their order, and deliver it to them.

Like the grocery delivery services, you dictate your schedule, letting the company know when you are available to work. Some of the more popular services are Grubhub (grubhub.com) and DoorDash (doordash.com). Grubhub drivers make $0.50 per mile (from restaurant to customer) plus tips. According to Glassdoor. com,[10] Grubhub drivers average about $12 per hour. For ten hours a week, that's more than $500 per month.

Deliver Stuff

Amazon is shortening its delivery time by employing people just like you. They call it Amazon Flex (flex.amazon.com). Like the service above, you simply state the hours you want to work, and they connect you with delivery needs. Deliverers drive to an Amazon site, pick up ordered items, and deliver the items to customers. According to Flex.Amazon.com,[11] drivers make between $18 and $25 per hour. On the low end, that's more than $800 per month, assuming ten hours per week.

You just found almost $10,000 of additional income for the year working ten hours per week!

Like most things in life, going the pretty well-known route has its strengths and weaknesses. The strength lies in the ability to plug into an existing system. Uber already has the mechanism for finding customers. You don't have to search for customers; they bring them to you. You also know, fairly well, how much you are going to get paid. The agreement is in place. The downside is that you have limited room for creativity and increases in income beyond working more hours. Regardless, these opportunities are worth considering.

+	**—**
Flexibility	Limited income growth
Existing system	Limited creativity
Immediate income	Must be self-disciplined

Gigs for Opportunity Makers

Driving people around? Hosting people at my house? Delivering groceries, Taco Bell Crunchwraps, and other random stuff? These are good, legitimate opportunities to find more money. But those of you who are more entrepreneurial and creative, you might desire other ways to make money.

There are reasons why people choose the be-your-own-business gig route. First, it allows individuals to express their passions and display their skills. Second, there is a significantly higher income potential compared to other opportunities. And we will spend some time discussing how to increase your income in the upcoming chapters. With Shipt or Amazon Flex, other than putting in more hours, you have limited control on how much money you can make.

+	**−**
Flexibility	No existing system
Express passion and skill	No assurance of income
No income limit	Slow income growth

People all over the nation are finding ways to become their own businesses. You probably know a few. They are using their passion and skill to make money. Let me throw out a few ideas for you.

Handyman

Are you good at fixing things around the house? Are neighbors and friends often asking you to come over to fix a toilet or install a light? Working as a handyman can be a good gig to earn additional income.

Music Teacher

Piano, guitar, violin—any type of music teacher. If you are skilled at playing an instrument and able to convey that knowledge to others, teaching music on the side may be a solid opportunity for you. If this is you, focus on teaching children. This is where you will find the majority of your students.

Consultant

Do you have experience in a particular field and like helping others succeed? Being a consultant may be your gig. I know several experienced pastors who provide consulting services to other church leaders. They provide an outsider's perspective on internal challenges.

Fitness Trainer

Do you find yourself at the gym on a regular basis? Do you enjoy working out? Fitness trainers help individuals pursue their physical health goals. They typically get paid hourly or by the session. Some trainers are independent while others partner with a particular gym. You would need to calculate which option provides the best opportunity to increase your income.

Make Stuff

Etsy (etsy.com) provides an incredible platform to sell handcrafted products. Do you like to craft? Do you like to work with wood? Has someone seen one of your creations and said, "Hey, can you make me one?" If so, selling your creations on Etsy may be an opportunity for you.

Find Stuff and Sell It

Craigslist (craigslist.com) and eBay (ebay.com) provide platforms where you can sell just about anything. If rummaging through yard sales makes you feel like a pirate looking for hidden treasure, these may be good options for you. At yard sales and thrift stores, look for items of value that are being sold on the cheap and buy them. After purchasing the items, sell them on eBay or Craigslist for an amount greater than the purchase price. The profit is yours to keep.

One way to express your passion through this is to search and sell items that interest and excite you. For example, if you love baseball memorabilia, you could specialize in searching and selling those types of items. This will also allow you to become a trusted seller due to the consistency of the sale items.

I hope the gigs we've covered so far are getting you excited about finding more money. It may be that none of these fit you perfectly, but hopefully they help bring to mind something that is. Opportunities abound! You've just got to get a little creative and find them.

Important Websites for Side Giggers

John needs a new website for his company. The Wonder Company needs someone to take their customer service calls. Dana needs someone to install a recently purchased ceiling fan. Katie's business is taking off, and she needs a virtual assistant. Art just wrote a book, but it desperately needs some editing.

Where do people go to find someone to help with these tasks? They could ask their immediate network of family, friends, and coworkers. But that often leads to a bunch of dead ends. They don't have time to wait until someone with the right skill set crosses their path. They need help now.

More and more people are turning to websites that connect individuals who want a gig with people and companies who need a service. I have put together a list of sites that you should check out. These sites connect people who want side income with those who will provide it. Some on these sites are specifically looking for certain skills, but not all. (Due to the constantly changing and growing nature of the gig economy, it's likely that some of these will have changed by the time you're reading this book and that countless more will have been created.)

Sites presenting opportunities for a wide range of skills:[12]

> Steady.com
>
> Upwork.com
>
> Guru.com
>
> SimplyHired.com
>
> FlexJobs.com
>
> ratracerebellion.com
>
> Freelancer.com
>
> WAHM.com
>
> Solidgigs.com

Sites primarily presenting opportunities for those with digital and writing skills:

> LocalSolo.com
>
> Behance.net
>
> Fiverr.com
>
> toptal.com
>
> mturk.com
>
> Cloudpeeps.com
>
> servicescape.com
>
> 99designs.com

Sites presenting opportunities for those with handyman skills:

> TaskRabbit.com

Takl.com

Thumbtack.com

Zaarly.com

Homeadvisor.com

Houzz.com

Sites presenting opportunities for those with administrative skills:

Belaysolutions.com

Timeetc.com

Clickworker.com

Zirtual.com

Worldwide101.com

Sites presenting opportunities for those with educator skills:

wyzant.com

vipkid.com

tutor.com

chegg.com

takelessons.com (for music educators)

teachparttime.com

dadaabc.com

Working Your *Find More Money* Workflow

A number of side gigs are available for both opportunity takers and opportunity makers. In this chapter we have barely scratched the surface. Take another look at your passions and skills. Then start exploring the opportunities available. Your side gig is out there, waiting for you to find it.

Take some time to consider a side gig that aligns with your passions and skills.

First, write down the passions you identified from the prior step. Then write down opportunities that may align with those passions.

Passion 1: _____   **Opportunity 1:** _____

Passion 2: _____   **Opportunity 2:** _____

Passion 3: _____   **Opportunity 3:** _____

Next, write down the skills you identified in the prior step. Do the same thing. Consider opportunities that may align with your skills.

Skill 1: _____   **Opportunity 1:** _____

Skill 2: _____   **Opportunity 2:** _____

Skill 3: _____   **Opportunity 3:** _____

Do any opportunities appear on both lists? If so, you may have found your side gig.

Find more money.
Get financially healthy.
Advance God's kingdom among the rich.

STEP 6

Know Your Business

"Okay. . . . Got it. . . . I should be able to be there on Thursday evening. Hey, thank you for your help."

Austin hung up the phone as Brooklyn was dragging herself into the kitchen. Her eyes were squinting, adjusting to the light. It was 6:00 a.m. on Tuesday.

"Who in the world were you talking to?" Brooklyn asked. She noticed that the coffeepot contained a fresh batch of coffee. "And thank you for making the coffee." She opened a cabinet above their counter and reached for a mug.

"That was Cary," answered Austin.

Brooklyn yawned. "What was so important that you had to talk to him this early?" She poured her coffee, added a bit of creamer, and sat down at their small round kitchen table.

"He sent me a text last night," replied Austin. "He said he had a few ideas for me, lessons he had learned. Plus, he had someone I might be able to help. Early morning was the only time he could talk today."

Brooklyn started looking for bread. Her regular breakfast was fairly ordinary—coffee and toast. "Have you seen the bread?"

"I think it's by the chips in the cupboard."

Austin pulled out his laptop and placed it on the kitchen table. "Cary said that one of the first things we need to do is consider what type of business we are."

"What type of business we are at 6:00 a.m. in the morning?" questioned Brooklyn.

Austin took out his computer and began typing. "It doesn't have to be complicated. And it might help us save money on our taxes."

Brooklyn looked at Austin as she placed two slices of bread in the toaster. "Austin, we barely have any taxes. Remember, we don't make that much money."

Austin had to agree. They never really owed much, if anything, for taxes.

"Well, we still need to set up and track everything correctly," noted Austin. "Since this is more than a hobby for us, we'll both be sole proprietors."

Brooklyn held up her arms. "Look at me! I'm a businesswoman! At 6:00 a.m.!"

Austin smiled. "You're about to be."

The toast popped up. Brooklyn placed the slices on her plate. "So, who is the client Cary was giving you?"

Austin had a slight smile. "You won't believe it. His name is Ben. I knew him in high school. And God had actually been placing him on my heart. I don't know why, but I can't help but think this has something to do with it."

Brooklyn took a sip of coffee. "Wow. Strong coffee."

"Good coffee is chewable coffee," Austin joked.

Brooklyn's tongue hung out of her mouth. "Gross. Can you hand me some more creamer?"

Getting Down to Business (Type)

Mama Needs Subscription Box, LLC knows exactly what moms need. How? Jenn is one.

Jenn is a highly creative friend of mine who went through some challenging times. In a span of three months, Jenn and her husband changed careers, moved to a new state, and had their third child. And you thought your last few months were busy. Soon after, she found herself neglecting her own well-being, something to which many moms can relate. Though the journey was long, Jenn eventually found herself with her head above water and filled with a newfound sense of hope and peace.

Jenn did not want her challenges to go to waste. She wanted to use her God-given creativity and experience to help others and increase her family's income. Through prayer and brainstorming, Mama Needs Subscription Box was born. Jenn set up a limited liability company (LLC), and she was off.

Mama Needs Subscription Box is the self-care subscription company Jenn wished was available to her during the difficult times she experienced, encouraging her to take time and care for herself. Jenn is now a busy mom and business owner, using her passion and skill to create an opportunity that helps others and finds more money.

Business Types in the Gig Economy

Jenn created a limited liability company. Should you?

Questions like this can cause many to run away from side gigging. Somewhere along the way they've convinced themselves that their brains are not capable of understanding this type of information. They are intimidated. Others are afraid of making the wrong decision. They don't want to end up in federal prison because they chose an LLC when they should have chosen a sole proprietorship.

If you can relate to these concerns, let me encourage you to follow Bobby McFerrin's suggestion: "Don't worry, be happy."[1] Here is the reality—you *can* understand this information, and you *can* make the right decision. And you won't go to federal prison if you happen to choose the wrong business type—at least, you shouldn't.

Independent Contractors

Are you driving for Uber? Do you deliver groceries for Shipt.com? Do you deliver stuff for Amazon.com?

If so, you are probably an independent contractor, which means you are self-employed. A large chunk of gig economy workers are independent contractors.

The status of independent contractor primarily relates to the way you receive income.

Independent contractors are nonemployees of companies. They perform services or produce outcomes under a contract with a company, but they have significant discretion on how to perform the services or produce the outcomes.

If you are an independent contractor for your gig, you are receiving self-employed income. Since you are a nonemployee, the company through which you are contracted will probably send you a 1099, depending on the amount of income you make. You will not receive a W-2. And taxes are not deducted from your payment.

Independent contractors are able to pursue a variety of business types for tax and legal purposes. If you choose not to set up a business type, you will essentially pay taxes in a way similar to sole proprietorships—filing a Schedule C along with your 1040.

What are sole proprietorships? I'm glad you asked.

Sole Proprietorships

A sole proprietorship is a single-person business. Your business is just me, myself, and I. Often, sole proprietorships are under the person's name, but not always. If you have business revenue and expenses that you are tracking outside of your household revenue and expenses, you probably have a sole proprietorship on your hands.

Reasons Side Giggers Choose Sole Proprietorships

- Sole proprietorships are easy to set up. If you choose to use a name other than your personal name, you will likely need to register the name with your state. Once you have your name, set up a business checking account, and congratulations on your new business!
- Setting up a sole proprietorship is incredibly cheap. There are very few costs associated with getting the business set up.

- Taxes are fairly simple for sole proprietorships. You just claim the gains or losses on your individual tax returns using Schedule C.

Downsides of Sole Proprietorships

- You don't have any legal protection. This is, by far, the biggest weakness. You are fully liable for a sole proprietorship. There is no protective barrier between business and personal. If your sole proprietorship gets sued, you are personally getting sued.
- You are personally liable for all debts of the business.
- It can be difficult to raise funds or get loans for the business. If you are thinking that either are necessary for your business, a sole proprietorship may not be right for you.

Basic Steps for Starting Your Sole Proprietorship

If you've decided to create a sole proprietorship, congratulations! Many in the gig economy have gone this route. Setting up a sole proprietorship is fairly simple. Here are typical steps in the creation of this business type, but please be sure to check with your state to ensure you are abiding by their requirements.

Here is your sole proprietorship creation checklist:

1. Pick a business name. Some just use their personal name. If you decide to use a fictitious name (not your personal name), make sure no one else in your state is using it. I also recommend checking whether the web domain is available.
2. Purchase your web domain, even if you think you won't need it.

3. Register the business name with your state. Your name is a DBA, "doing business as," because you are doing business as the fictitious name.

4. Get your Employer Identification Number (EIN). You can start with your Social Security number. But if you decide to hire someone, you will need an EIN. You can apply for an EIN at irs.gov.

5. Open a business checking account. This will help you keep your personal transactions separate from business transactions.

6. Make sure you have all the licenses and permits necessary to do the business. Some side gigs require business licenses. Check to see if you need a license to do your side gig.

You may now be thinking, *But Jenn set up an LLC. What's that?* Good question. Let's take a look at another popular business type in the gig economy—the Limited Liability Company.

Limited Liability Company (LLC)

Jenn created an LLC for Mama Needs Subscription Box. In the gig economy LLCs are also popular. It is called a Limited Liability Company because, unlike a sole proprietorship, this business type provides a barrier between your personal assets and your business assets. It limits your liability. If you think you may be at risk for a lawsuit, an LLC is a good option.

Reasons Side Giggers Choose LLCs

- You work in a creative industry that inherently makes you liable to lawsuits.

- You have some degree of protection. This is the main reason people set up LLCs for their gigs. An LLC creates a barrier between a person and a business. While the business can experience lawsuits, these suits don't necessarily impact the individual.
- You are not personally liable for business debts.
- Obtaining loans and raising funds are easier (though not necessarily easy) with LLCs.
- Taxes are not overly complex. You just file a Schedule C with your personal income taxes.

Some Downsides of LLCs

- Setting up an LLC is more cumbersome when compared to a sole proprietorship. More paperwork is involved.
- Set-up and ongoing costs are higher than a sole proprietorship.
- Reporting is sometimes required. You may have to file annual reports for your LLC.

Basic Steps for Starting Your LLC

Creating an LLC is going to be slightly more cumbersome than creating a sole proprietorship. However, you will still find it very doable. Don't get intimidated by the paperwork. Remember, millions of individuals have created LLCs, and you can too. If you can do a gig, you can create an LLC. Here are some typical steps, but like creating a sole proprietorship, check with your state guidelines first. Each state's requirements can vary.

Here is your LLC creation checklist:

1. Get your state's article of incorporation forms for LLCs.

2. Pick a business name. Like the sole proprietorship, check to make sure no one else is using it. Also, check to see if any potential web domains are available.

3. Purchase your web domain.

4. Choose the registered agent for the LLC. Most states require a registered agent. This is the person who will receive legal papers for the LLC. More than likely, that person is you.

5. Fill out and file the articles of incorporation.

6. Get your Employer Identification Number (EIN) on irs.gov.

7. Create an operating agreement. Not all states require an operating agreement, but it is good to have nonetheless. This document outlines the responsibilities and rights of LLC members. If it is just you, this document will be fairly simple.

8. Publicize your company (if required). Some states require that you announce—often referred to as a public notice—the creation of your company. If your state requires this, follow the state's guidelines on how to do it.

9. Make sure you have all the licenses and permits necessary for the business.

Now there are various types of LLCs, typically defined by ownership structure. Each one has its strengths and weaknesses, so be sure to study each one to see which best fits your needs. Two common structures are single-owner LLCs and multi-owner LLCs. For tax purposes, single-owner LLCs are treated like sole proprietorships (Schedule C). Multi-owner LLCs are treated like partnerships, where all members report their share of profits on their personal tax returns.

Which One Is Right for You?

So, which one is right for you? It depends. There are several reasons some choose the sole proprietorship route over the LLC route and vice versa. Here are a few questions that may help clarify your route.

How Many Business Owners Are There?

If the answer is "more than one," LLC is the route for you. If the answer is "one," either can work.

Do Personal Assets Need Protection?

If you are concerned about protecting your assets, LLC is the route for you. Unlike a sole proprietorship, LLCs provide a barrier between your assets and the business's assets. People can sue the business, not you.

Can I Afford LLC Filing Costs?

While the costs for filing an LLC aren't extremely high, the comparative costs for filing a sole proprietorship are lower. Check with your state's filing costs for LLCs. If the filing costs are too high for you, the sole proprietorship route may be best.

Get Your Business Going

For opportunity makers and opportunity takers, sole proprietorships and LLCs have been used extensively to find more money. If your gig is a new business, consider the strengths and weaknesses of both. And consider which best fits you, your business, and your goals. Of course, it is always best to consult with a tax professional to ensure you are making the best decision for you and your business.

Find more money.
Get financially healthy.
Advance God's kingdom among the poor.

STEP 7

Get Organized

Austin was leaning back in his office chair behind his desk when someone knocked on the door. It startled him to the point where he almost fell over backwards. He wasn't expecting anyone. But then again, that's the life of a minister.

"Come in," yelled Austin.

The door opened and in came Cary.

"Hey, Austin!" greeted Cary. "I just wanted to stop in and check on you. How has today been?"

Austin thought for a moment. "Incredible."

"Really?" Cary responded enthusiastically. "Tell me about it."

Austin placed his elbows on the desk and leaned forward. "It seems like almost every day I get to witness something firsthand that is amazing, something only God can do."

"You have my attention," smiled Cary. He sat down in a chair on the other side of Austin's desk.

"Well, I won't give you the names, but there was a marriage that was on the verge of divorce six months ago. They had already separated. But after six months of ministering to them and allowing God to work in their lives, they're back together, not considering divorce, and committed to pursuing oneness in their marriage."

"That is awesome!" responded Cary.

"And then, about two hours ago, I went to the high school where a few of our students attend. I joined them for lunch. While we were eating, the conversation turned to the gospel. And right there one of the students trusted Jesus as his Lord and Savior!"

"Wow," exclaimed Cary. "So it *has* been a good day."

Cary looked around the office. "You really don't want to leave this church, do you?"

"No," Austin sighed. "It's amazing what God's doing here."

Cary nodded his head. "You need to get organized."

Austin wasn't sure how to take Cary's statement.

"Look, I know my office doesn't look neat right now, but I usually clean up before I leave," Austin said apologetically.

"Not your office," corrected Cary. "Your side gig. If you want to make the most of your side gig, you have to get organized. Trust me. Without organization, your side gig will become a burden, not a blessing."

Austin quickly understood how side gigs could create a mess if he and Brooklyn weren't careful. It was another item on the schedule and more money to manage.

"Look," said Cary. "I'm able to have a successful side gig because I plan, schedule, and track. I want you to keep your job. I don't want you to quit. So you and Brooklyn need to start planning, scheduling, and tracking now."

Cary stood up and gave Austin a fist bump. "Take care, man," said Cary.

"You, too," replied Austin. "Oh, and thanks again for sending Ben my way. I look forward to helping him."

Cary smiled and walked out of the office. Just then Austin's phone buzzed. Brooklyn had sent him a text. It read, "Officially approved as shopper. Time to find more money!"

Successful Gigs Are Organized Gigs

Our God is a God of order.

"Since God is not a God of disorder but of peace" (1 Cor. 14:33). Paul is writing of the need for order in worship services. The presence of order in worship brings God glory because it reflects who he is.

To further reflect his character, God has designed you for order. You work best when chaos is minimized and order is present. We all do. In whatever you do, pursuing order usually creates less stress and better results.

A. A. Milne, the author of *Winnie-the-Pooh*, once said, "Organizing is what you do before you do something, so that when you do it, it is not all mixed up."

Benjamin Franklin said, "For every minute spent organizing, an hour is earned."

Clayton would agree with Milne and Franklin.

Clayton is another one of my friends who embarked on the journey to find more money. He is a driven disciple, working hard and trusting God with the results. His wife worked full-time while he was a full-time, masters-level student. Like many, they were victims of undergraduate student loans. It crushed their ability to give and save. Though Clayton was in school full-time, he knew he needed to help with their finances. So he found a gig.

Clayton joined a local pet-sitting service provider. He liked pets, but they really weren't his passion. Regardless, it was an opportunity, and Clayton took it.

Balancing school and the gig was a challenge. Pet sitting doesn't allow you to have a consistent schedule, so Clayton had to excel at organization. And this is true for most side giggers.

Side gigs add new potential disrupters to your life. If your life is a chaotic mess right now, a side gig will not help the mess.

Organization will help your ability to reach your income goal. We're going to focus on five specific areas that need organization so that you can find more money.

1. Workflow
2. Schedule
3. Pricing
4. Money
5. Meeting Place

Let's check out each one.

Organize Your Workflow

You know what a workflow is. You are in the midst of one right now. A workflow consists of sequential steps that help you reach your goal. Your workflow tells you, for each goal, what must be done to reach that goal, step by step. For example, if your goal is to get a cheeseburger from McDonald's, the workflow may look something like this:

Step 1: Get into car.
Step 2: Drive car to McDonald's drive-through.

Step 3. When prompted by employee, request cheeseburger.

Step 4: Pay employee at window.

Step 5: Receive cheeseburger from employee.

That is your McDonald's cheeseburger workflow. Now, go ahead and enjoy that cheeseburger. You deserve it.

Why are workflows important? Workflows break goals into smaller, more doable tasks. Workflows can make the impossible seem possible, the daunting seem doable.

As a side gigger, you're going to have a number of goals, both big and small. And using workflows can keep you on track and help you achieve those goals.

There are two types of workflows to consider—single-use workflows and standardized workflows. A single-use workflow can help you launch your new gig or help you reach a new goal. Standardized workflows keep the side gig going by helping maintain consistency, which is incredibly important for customers. For opportunity makers, a standardized workflow can help you ensure consistent experiences, services, or products.

Are you wondering how to create your first workflow? Great. Here is a workflow for developing workflows.

A Workflow for Workflows

❏ Step 1: Identify your goal.
❏ Step 2: Name your workflow (so you don't confuse it with other workflows).
❏ Step 3: Brainstorm tasks needed to reach your goal.
❏ Step 4: Sequentially order the tasks.

❏ Step 5: If possible, include the expected time required for each task.

❏ Step 6: Make sure everyone who needs the workflow has a copy.

❏ Step 7: Take the steps and reach the goal!

Workflows are important for opportunity takers and opportunity makers alike. Even if you are an Uber or Lyft driver, ensuring you have a standardized workflow to ensure an excellent rider experience will go a long way toward increasing your income.

Ride-Share Experience Workflow

❏ 1. Get out, open door, and help with any luggage.

❏ 2. Greet rider with a smile.

❏ 3. Once in car, verify destination.

❏ 4. Offer bottle of water.

❏ 5. Ask for music preference. Use music playlist that aligns with preference.

❏ 6. Ask if passenger needs the air conditioner to be cooler or hotter. Adjust accordingly.

❏ 7. Try to engage in conversation. If passenger seems resistant, stop talking.

❏ 8. Upon arrival, thank passenger and open the door.

Create and organize your workflows. They can be instrumental in your success, maximizing your ability to capture and retain customers.

Go ahead and create your first workflow below. I've given you up to ten steps. If you need more, feel free to use the margins.

❏ Step 1: _____

❏ Step 2: _____

❏ Step 3: _____

❏ Step 4: _____

❏ Step 5: _____

❏ Step 6: _____

❏ Step 7: _____

❏ Step 8: _____

❏ Step 9: _____

❏ Step 10: _____

Organize Your Schedule

"Your greatest danger is letting the urgent things crowd out the important."[1] —Charles E. Hummel

In 1967, Charles E. Hummel wrote a classic work, *The Tyranny of the Urgent*, about an issue we all face—the urgent taking precedence over the important. The timelessness of the work speaks to the timelessness of the problem. The demands of others and inner compulsions fill up our schedules. When they do, we find ourselves unable to do anything else. We are busy doing tasks that are not the most important.

"I'm just too busy."

I have heard many who desire to find more income say these four words. And they are probably right—they are too busy. Every day their schedule is filled. But often it is not filled by them but rather by others and unexpected urgent needs.

> **The tyranny of the urgent siphons out time to find more money. How do you combat this consumer of time?**

The tyranny of the urgent siphons out time to find more money. How do you combat this consumer of time?

You take control of your schedule. Here are some suggestions to do just that:

Plan Your Month before It Starts

You don't accomplish what you don't plan. Successful side giggers are expert planners. They also know that you don't accidently find time to have a side gig. It takes intentionality. It takes planning.

Map out each month before the first hits. Schedule as much as possible. The more you schedule, the less likely the tyranny of the urgent can take over. Here are some categories to consider placing on your calendar:

- Bible devotional time
- Work hours and tasks
- Side gig hours and tasks
- Family time and activities

- School-related activities
- Extracurricular activities
- Household tasks
- Personal finance to-dos
- Time off

Control your calendar. Do not let the tyranny of the urgent take over.

Create a Daily To-Do List (the Day Before)

You have your monthly schedule. This gives you a good aerial view of your plan to hit your money goal. Now you need a daily plan. While referring to your monthly schedule, consider what needs to happen tomorrow.

I have a prioritized to-do list. Both small and large tasks are on there. It is a list I consistently update and prioritize. I often use an app on my phone, but sometimes I just use a piece of paper. Use whatever medium works for you.

If you have not tested the to-do list waters, I encourage you to do so. Find an app on your phone that is easy to use. There are some good options out there. Or use a piece of paper—whatever works for you. I believe you will find it to be a useful tool that helps bring a sense of clarity, increased productivity, and a way to make sure you have time for your gig.

Exchange Time Wasters for Production Makers

According to the Bureau of Labor Statistics,[2] Americans spend an average of 2.8 hours per day watching television. We are mesmerized by screens, literally spending hours mindlessly watching our televisions, computers, and phones.

Replace time wasters like these with side gig work. If you are like the average American, the hours needed to find more money are available to you. You just need to turn mindless activities into money-making activities.

Organize Your Pricing (and Profit)

This will mostly pertain to opportunity makers. Opportunity takers usually have little control over the amount they can charge for a service. There may be some flexibility but not much. However, opportunity makers have significant control over their pricing, which can be both a blessing and a burden.

Determining a price should be a thoughtful and flexible process. Simply throwing a price tag out there can result in no sales or no profit (Revenue – Expenses = Profit), neither of which is good for those needing to find more money.

To start, know your expenses. There are two types of expenses—*fixed* and *variable.*

Fixed expenses are those you are going to pay no matter what—website costs, any subscriptions, etc. It doesn't matter whether you have one or one hundred customers; fixed costs are constant. Hopefully your fixed costs are low.

Variable expenses are those that increase or decrease, depending on the number of customers. For example, if you decide to start carving slate cutting boards, competing with Andrew, your slate costs will increase as more customers request your cutting boards. You must buy more slate to meet the demand.

To make profit, your price for each cutting board must be greater than their variable costs and a portion of the fixed costs. To break even, or to lose money, puts you in a worse place than before.

Let me provide some simplified slate cutting board costs:

Variable Costs	
Slate for cutting boards	$10
Fixed Costs	
Website	$25 per month
Tools	$25 average per month

Now let's say that you decide to ascribe $5 of the website and tool costs to each customer. Here is what your break-even point looks like.

Slate for cutting boards	$10
Website	$5
Tools	$5
Breakeven Point	**$20**

Your break-even point is $20. Therefore, to make profit, your price per cutting board must be greater than $20. How much greater? It depends. Investigate your competition. What are their prices? Unless you can offer something significantly different, you likely won't be able to charge much more, and you won't want to charge way less.

There is a balance. If you are too expensive, no one will buy what you are selling. But if you are too cheap, you won't make a profit, and, counterintuitively, people may not buy your product because the cheap price implies it is cheaply made. So carefully consider your pricing. Determining your price is a blessing and a burden, and you may need to adjust it until you find your sweet spot.

Organize Your Money

I know. This part probably terrifies you. You have struggled with your personal finances and are wondering how you can even think about managing your side-gig finances. Don't worry, you can do this. You just need to keep it simple.

Here are five suggestions to get you started.

I. Open a Business Checking Account

Get a business checking account with its own checks and debit card. These are easy to set up. Don't try to mingle your business finances with your personal finances. It will get too complex, and you will go crazy.

2. Keep Track of Your Invoices

For made-to-order products or services, these are especially important. Invoices are records of sale. An invoice should have three essential elements—what the purchaser receives, how much he owes, and when he owes it. Invoice records help you get paid on time and reduce arguments over billing. Make sure the purchaser agrees to the invoice prior to starting any made-to-order work.

3. Keep Track of Your Expenses

Keeping track of your expenses will help you in two ways. First, you will know whether you are making any profit. Second, you will know how much you can potentially write off and deduct on your taxes.

Here's a quick example using basic numbers:

> Let's say you make and sell jewelry on Etsy. Your costs to make the jewelry totaled $100. Unfortunately, your sales struggled, and you only made $90 in sales. So you lost $10.
>
> If you didn't keep track of your expenses, you increased your personal taxable income by $90, the amount of your sales.
>
> If you kept track of your expenses, the impact on your taxes is a potential $10 deduction on taxable income, the amount you lost on your sales. You may also be able to write off the expenses (up to $100) associated with the side gig.

Needless to say, keeping track of your expenses is a smart money decision.

4. Set Aside Money for Taxes

If you are making money on your side gig, which I hope you are, you will need to set aside money for taxes. I recommend setting aside 35 percent of your side gig income for taxes. If you think you will owe $1,000 or more, you should pay your taxes every three months (four times each year). The IRS Form 1040-ES will help you with this.

5. Have People Pay the Business, Not You

If your business has a name other than your personal name, make sure people use the business name for their payments. This is another step to make sure you keep your business finances separate from your personal finances.

Organize Your Meeting Place

Before you launch your side gig, you have one more vital element to organize—your meeting place.

If an emergency were to happen at or to our house, our boys know where to find us. We set up a designated meeting place and remind them of that place on a regular basis. We want our boys to know where to find us.

And you need your customers to know where to find you and your offerings. As you promote your side gig, you will need to send potential customers somewhere. For many opportunity makers, this is a website. The website doesn't need to be elaborate, just attractive and professional. Opportunity makers can also use sites like Etsy or eBay as their meeting place, depending on their side gig. Just make sure that, like a website, your business page is attractive and professional.

Opportunity takers will primarily use their company's website. The main concern for opportunity takers is to ensure that their profile looks happy and professional. Grumpy, sloppy profiles don't scream, "Use me for this service!"

Organizing your workflows, schedule, pricing, money, and meeting place are essential elements to your ability to find more money. This is true for opportunity makers and opportunity takers.

Our God is not a God of chaos. Reflect order in your life. Get organized.

Now let's look at how you tell everyone about your side gig.

Find more money.
Get financially healthy.
Advance God's kingdom through your church.

STEP 8

Overcommunicate

Ding! Ding!

"What was that?" asked Austin.

Austin and Brooklyn were back at their townhouse. Brooklyn was eating a piece of leftover marble cake from the gender reveal party.

With a mouthful of cake, she responded, "My side gig!" A few crumbs of marble cake shot out of her mouth and onto Austin's shirt. She covered her mouth and giggled.

Austin slowly brushed the crumbs off his shirt. "Umm. . . . Can you try that again without the crumb shower?"

Brooklyn laughed and finished the bite of cake.

"I'm sorry," she said. "The company's app notifies me when I have a delivery scheduled. I just put in my availability for tomorrow, and now they're matching me with people who want their groceries picked up and delivered."

Brooklyn grabbed her phone, opened up the app, and handed the phone to Austin.

"See," she said proudly. "I already have three deliveries scheduled for tomorrow. I'm a wanted shopper."

Austin was impressed. She had just been approved by the company to be a shopper, and now she already had three deliveries. Brooklyn really was already on her way to making more money.

Unlike him.

He looked at his phone. There was no request for his services. Austin began to think that maybe Brooklyn was right. Maybe being a handyman wasn't the way to go, given how quickly they needed the money. Nobody even knew he had a side gig, if you could call it that at this point.

"Hey, I think I want to give Cary a quick call," Austin said to Brooklyn.

"Okay," Brooklyn smiled. "I wanted to finish off this cake anyway. I'm doing it for the baby."

Austin gave her a slight grin and shook his head. He walked to their bedroom, shut the door, and called Cary. Cary picked up.

"Hey, Cary. It's Austin. I think I may have a little problem. How can I make money from a side gig that nobody knows exists?"

Austin listened intently to Cary for several minutes. "Uh-huh. . . . Right. . . . Elevator pitch. . . . I agree. . . . I can check on those lists. . . . Community pages. . . . Got it. . . . I think my friends would be happy to help. . . . Yes. . . . Okay. . . . Overcommunicate. . . . Thank you. . . . I will let you know."

Austin hung up the phone and walked out of the bedroom. He grabbed his laptop, placed it on the table, and started working.

Brooklyn looked over at Austin. "What are you doing?"

"Making sure people know I exist," replied Austin.

Top-of-Mind Awareness

While reading this list, take note of which brand pops into your mind first.

Fast food

Insurance

Soda

Bookstore

Bank

Pharmacy

Coffee

Car

Truck

University

Grocery store

Lawn mower

Top-of-mind awareness—how promptly a brand, product, or service comes to mind. Brands strive to be the number one spot in your mind for their category. The brands that came to mind as you read the list have worked hard to secure that top spot in your brain.

A coffee shop near me just closed. They were only open for about six months. Admittedly, I was part of the problem. When I thought about coffee, they never came to mind, even though they were the closest coffee shop to me. I only thought about them as I passed by their shop on the way to another.

They never secured a spot in my brain.

When you start your side gig, you have two promotional goals—create awareness and create *top-of-mind* awareness. The first will announce the arrival of your side gig. The second will increase your income. I knew the coffee shop existed. I was aware. But I never bought a cup of coffee from them. It wasn't because I didn't like their coffee but because when I wanted coffee, they never came to mind. They had not achieved top-of-mind awareness.

Awareness of your side gig will come from communication. Top-of-mind awareness will come from overcommunication.

Your Key to Successful Promotion—Overcommunication

Communication does a poor job of communicating. Overcommunication is what truly communicates.

You may be scratching your head. But consider this—how many times has someone told you about a service he provides, yet you completely forget about him and his service. Or how many people, representing their companies, have knocked on your door to sell you their services? Now, how many of those company names can you actually remember?

Telling someone once about your side gig will not create the type of awareness you need to increase your income. Sending one email or having one Facebook post will not accomplish your goals.

As you embark on this step of your workflow, think repetition. Promotion is not a one-time action. Your initial promotions create awareness. They proclaim to the world that your gig exists. But this will not result in ongoing side income. You will have to go through this step over and over and over again. You will have to overcommunicate.

You are constantly thinking about your side gig. They are not. As you overcommunicate, keep this in mind—the moment you get sick of promoting your side gig is often the exact moment people start realizing you have a side gig.

Communication does a poor job of communicating. Overcommunication is what truly communicates.

> The moment you get sick of promoting your side gig is often the exact moment people start realizing you have a side gig.

Promoting Your Gig

Some side gigs limit your ability to promote your services. For example, Uber riders are not able to select specific drivers. It doesn't make sense to promote your services outside the application. There are some internal ways you can promote yourself. And we will talk about those shortly.

But for many side giggers, the ability to promote is wide open. Even for those who partner with a company like Airbnb, promotion can be a lynchpin to increasing your income. Airbnb will promote *their* site, *their* company. But it is up to you to push *your* rental.

We're going to look at a few essential elements you should have in your promotional repertoire. So, whether you're an opportunity taker or an opportunity maker, consider how these elements can help your side gig's initial awareness, and eventual top-of-mind awareness, to generate income for you.

Essential Element I: Your Elevator Pitch

How excited are you to listen to a thirty-minute sales pitch? Neither is anybody else.

An elevator pitch is a fifteen- to thirty-second statement about you and your side gig. Elevator pitches help boil down the essentials of your side gig so you can promote the gig in a quick, easy-to-understand manner. So, if you have only an elevator ride to promote your side gig, you're ready to go.

Here are the elements of a successful elevator pitch.

1. Ask a question about a need. I like starting pitches with questions. They create intrigue and involvement. "Do you like good coffee?"

2. State who you are. If you have a separate business name, state your business name as well. "My name is Andrea Smith, and I own Neighborhood Coffee Café. We just opened."

3. State what you do. This should solve the problem created with your initial question. "We pride ourselves on making the best cup of coffee in town."

4. Tell them something unique about what you do. This is your differentiator. Other people or businesses probably offer similar services or products. You need to help them see why you or your business should be considered first. "We have an exclusive, top-rated coffee blend coffee lovers can't seem to get enough of."

5. Tell them what you want. You need to have a "call to action." They won't know their next step unless you tell them. "You should stop by the store today. Tell the barista I sent you to check us out."

6. Give them a way to contact you or the business. "Here, let me give you my card. It has our website address on it."

ELEVATOR PITCH

"Do you like good coffee?

"My name is Andrea Smith, and I own Neighborhood Coffee Café. We just opened. We pride ourselves on making the best cup of coffee in town. We have an exclusive, top-rated coffee blend coffee lovers can't seem to get enough of. You should stop by the store today. Tell the barista I sent you to check us out. Here, let me give you my card. It has our website address on it."

That would have been enough for me to try out the coffee shop that closed down. Elevator pitches are powerful promotional tools. Nail down your elevator pitch. It will help with verbal and written promotions.

Elevator pitches are valuable for both opportunity takers and opportunity makers. Here are pitches for an Airbnb rental provider (opportunity taker) and a handyman (opportunity maker).

ELEVATOR PITCH FOR AIRBNB RENTAL

"Do you need a relaxing weekend getaway?

"My name is Katie Rogers. I have an old, renovated farmhouse on our farm that we rent out. All you can hear are the birds and crickets chirping. It is so relaxing. I would love for you to be our guest one weekend. Here's the website where you can see pictures and reviews of the place."

ELEVATOR PITCH FOR A HANDYMAN

"Do you have a few home repairs that have been lingering for a while?

"My name is Bill Thornton, and I'm a handyman. I provide general house repair services, including drywall repair, leaking faucets, and painting. I do this after regular work hours and over the weekend. I find this is convenient for clients. Here is my card. Feel free to call or send me an email."

Now, it's your turn. Fill out the spaces below.

1. Ask a question about a need. _____

_____

2. State who you are. _____

_____

3. State what you do. _____

_____

4. Tell something unique about what you do. _____

_____

5. Tell what you want. _____

_____

6. Give a way to contact you or the business. _____

_____

Put it all together, and you have your elevator pitch!

Essential Element 2: Your Digital Presence

Even if the digital realm is not your thing, you should try to have some digital presence. About 50 percent of the global population[1] accesses the Internet for a variety of purposes, including looking for the product or services you offer. You need to make yourself and your side gig easy to find. Here are some suggestions.

Get on lists. Make sure your name or your business shows up on the lists people search for your services. For example, if you are a handyman, you need to be on Angie's List, Thumbtack, Takl, and Yelp. Find the trusted lists for the services you offer and get on them.

Get a website. A website can give you a significant credibility boost. The website doesn't need to be complex. Just make sure you have attractive examples of your work, endorsements, and contact information. You can create relatively inexpensive but appealing websites through sites like Wix.com and One.com.

Get on social media. New side giggers often ignore social media platforms like Facebook and Instagram. Don't be one of them. People regularly search social media sites for products and services. Both Facebook and Instagram allow businesses to set up accounts. Create an account. Regularly post images of your work and interesting information that pertains to your particular industry.

Essential Element 3: Going Old School

The digital world is important for promoting your side gig. But so are a few old school elements. Just because the digital world is alive doesn't mean that the print world is dead. In fact, as the world goes more digital, print stands out that much more.

Business cards. You gave a great elevator pitch. Now what? Hand out business cards. Make sure all of the important information is on the card. A business card is a great way to conclude an introduction.

Flyers. Use flyers for handouts and bulletin boards. These are more prominent than you may think. Keep your eye out for places where flyers are placed. Often you find these places at local businesses. If you do find a location where flyers are being used, ask the business owner if you can place your flyer there as well. Use your elevator pitch to introduce him or her to your side gig.

Personal notes. When you give someone information about your side gig, the other person often gives you information about his business. When you receive this information, hold on to it. One way to stand out in a crowd, to be remembered, is to write a handwritten, personal note. Simply state that you enjoyed meeting them and to let you know if you can help in the future. Include your business card, even if you've already given them one. A personal note will make you and your side gig memorable.

Essential Element 4: Your Network

You have a network of people around you. There are some with whom you are close, your best friends and family. And there are those to whom you are loosely acquainted, social media friends and others. This group is ground zero for your promotional efforts.

If you've noticed, I have already mentioned a few friends of mine who have side gigs. Do you know how I know about my friends' side gigs? They talk and write about their side gigs a lot. Which is good. Remember, overcommunicate.

When reaching out to your network, there are three different asks you can make—try, tell, and connect. Ask them to try your side gig. See if they like it. Ask them to tell others about it. And ask them to connect you to those who may be interested in what you have to offer.

There are also some outside your network whom you should be trying to get in your network—influencers. These are people who have significant sway over those you think may be most interested in your side gig. When you reach out to influencers, make sure you have something to offer them—maybe a free stay at your Airbnb rental. And yes, I am interested.

Essential Element 5: Free Promotion

As soon as you heard me talk about promotion, anxiety may have kicked in. You don't have the money to spend on promotion. Hence, why you picked up this book. If this is you, I have good news for you—promoting your side gig does not have to cost you anything. Even if you choose not to get business cards or pay for a website, there are a ton of free ways to promote your side gig.

Social media. Engaging in social media is a way to get your name and business out there. I have already mentioned getting a Facebook page and an Instagram account. Both are free. But view these as places you can point people to get a feel for your business.

Get involved in social media conversations pertinent to your service or product. You can do this through a simple search of related keywords on various social media sites. When the right opportunity presents itself, point people to your pages or accounts.

Community sites. Most cities and towns have their own community social media pages. I, along with several thousand other people, am a member of the Wake Forest, North Carolina, Community Facebook page. It is an amazing place for people to connect with local businesses and local businesses to connect with people.

My wife asked a simple question on the Wake Forest page: "Does anybody know someone who does built-in bookshelves?" I saw the post after forty-two people had already responded, many of whom were business owners. It was incredible.

If your community has a community page, use it. It can be a great free tool for you.

Essential Element 6: Lessons from the Best

My friend Ashley and her husband ran into an unforeseen financial emergency that resulted in unwanted debt. Their cars died one month after purchasing a home. More significantly, an extremely serious medical diagnosis created a pile of medical bills.

To help their family recover financially, Ashley got a side gig. She started dog sitting.

As I write this, Ashley is the top-rated dog sitter in our area on Rover.com. Literally, she is at the top of the list with a number one next to her name. Browse Ashley's profile and you will notice a few things: she is really good at taking care of dogs, and she is really good at promoting her side gig on Rover.com. Ashley has pictures of her house, yard, kids, and numerous dogs she's cared for. She has crafted a profile that makes anyone looking for pet sitting comfortable. If I had a dog, Fido would stay with Ashley while I traveled.

If you are interested in pet sitting through Rover.com, here is my recommendation—learn from Ashley, or whoever is the top dog sitter in your area. Study how they succeed, and implement your findings.

Don't be afraid to learn from those who are succeeding with similar gigs. This is especially true, but certainly not exclusively so, for those who have gigs that don't lend themselves to outside promotions (i.e., Uber). You need to consider how to appeal to customers within the platform itself.

Often you can see ratings and reviews of side giggers that contract with other companies like Airbnb, Rover, etc. Learn from them as well. See what people like about them. How does their profile presentation differ from yours? Implement what you learn.

Essential Element 7: Creativity

Be creative. Try different ways of promoting your side gig. Have fun with it. If one strategy doesn't yield results, try another. This is *your* side gig, so if you have a promotional idea, give it a shot!

Your Key to Successful Promotion—Overcommunication

No, you're not mistaken. That is the same section heading as above. I would be remiss if I didn't overcommunicate the importance of overcommunication, especially for side gigs. Use these essential promotional elements to create awareness about your gig. Use them over and over again to create top-of-mind awareness about your gig.

Strive to be the travel agent who immediately comes to mind when someone starts to think about a Disney vacation.

Strive to be the destination that immediately comes to mind when someone starts to think about a quick, weekend getaway.

Strive to be the website developer who immediately comes to mind when someone starts to think about their need for a website.

Strive to be the pet sitter who immediately comes to mind when someone needs to have their pets cared for.

Strive for awareness. And then strive for top-of-mind awareness.

Overcommunicate.

Overcommunicate.

And overcommunicate.

Find more money.
Get financially healthy.
Advance God's kingdom in your
neighborhood.

STEP 9

Create Fans

It was Wednesday evening and the church was buzzing with activity. The church held a few Bible study classes, choir practice, and kids and youth activities on Wednesday evenings. Austin had just finished teaching the middle school and high school students. The middle schoolers were running around acting crazy while the high schoolers tried to maintain their cool veneer. (The high schoolers did have a reputation to uphold, after all.)

"Hey, great evening!" encouraged Cary as he patted Austin on the back.

"Thanks," said Austin. "As always, I appreciate your being here."

Just then Sophia ran into the room and nearly tackled Cary. "Daddy!" she screamed.

"Whoa!" said a surprised Cary. "Good to see you too, honey."

With Sophia still holding on to him, Cary turned back to Austin. "You're helping Ben tomorrow, right?"

"I am," replied Austin. "I'm replacing a kitchen faucet."

"Perfect," smiled Cary. "Be sure to take before and after photos."

Austin had not thought about doing that. And he didn't quite understand why Cary recommended doing it.

Cary continued, "It's something I learned to do. Take the photos, and then send them in an email to the homeowner. It is amazing how often the homeowner then shares those photos on social media. Several people have contacted me after seeing their friend's photos and asking who the friend used."

"Wow," responded Austin. "That's a great idea. I have been letting people know that I do handyman work, but I've yet to receive any contacts."

"Well, it's only been a day since you starting promoting your side gig," comforted Cary. "Give it time. Here's the thing—deliver on expectations and provide an unexpected, small touch. I send them the photos and a handwritten thank-you note. It helps me to stand out and get more referrals."

Sophia jumped up and down and pulled out her notebook. "I know! Do what I do! I give people Bible verses. Just like this."

Sophia ripped a page out of her notebook and handed it to Austin. Austin looked at the paper. There was a verse on it.

> His master said to him, "Well done, good and faithful servant! You were faithful over a few things; I will put you in charge of many things. Share your master's joy!" (Matt. 25:21)

Austin quickly reflected on the verse. His heart needed to hear those words of Jesus. He smiled at the bright-eyed girl. "Thank you, Sophia. You have good ideas."

Austin turned to Cary. "I look forward to seeing Ben. I actually went to high school with him. It will be good to connect again."

Brooklyn walked up to the three. She looked at Cary. "Hey, I made $75 today by shopping for other people! And I have two more deliveries scheduled for tomorrow."

"That's great!" encouraged Cary.

Sophia thumbed through her notebook, pulled out a pen, and did some math. "That means, you only have $7,325 total left and $1,325 for the month left."

Brooklyn raised her eyebrows. She repeated Sophia, "*Only.*"

Go, Side Gig, Go!

What product or service are you a fan of? And why?

I like Starbucks coffee. I am a fan of their product. Why? Primarily consistency, as they always deliver on my expectations. But they also often provide me something small and unexpected, like a free coffee every now and then.

This means I am a fan. It also means that I bring others to my local Starbucks to partake in the experience.

I am also a big University of Kentucky athletics fan. This means that you don't have to drag me into talking about the Kentucky Wildcats. I do it unprompted. I wear the colors and cheer for them unashamedly.

Go, Cats.

You don't just want customers. You want fans, those who love what you offer and tell others about it. This is the key to long-term side-gig success.

How do you create fans?

It starts with trustworthiness. "But let your 'yes' mean 'yes,' and your 'no' mean 'no.' Anything more than this is from the evil one" (Matt. 5:37).

Yes means yes.

No means no.

This seems simple enough. Do what you said you would do.

God makes it clear that, as Christians, trustworthiness should mark our lives and our work; your side gig is not an exception.

Sometimes side gigs can get thrown to the back burner, other responsibilities crowding it out. And the expectations are not met. I have been on both ends of this, not meeting expectations and not having expectations met. Most of us have to some degree.

It is easy to, unintentionally, treat side-gig expectations as somehow less important.

But they are not.

They are not because, first and foremost, God doesn't provide a side-gig exclusion for trustworthiness. He calls us to integrity in all of life, even the things that seem the least significant.

But there's also a practical reason why side gigs aren't the exception to trustworthiness: because it only takes a few customers, talking to others about their experiences, to derail your ability to find more money.

All the work you've put into your side gig can be for naught by a simple, "This person (or business) cannot be trusted," type of review.

You can avoid this by managing and delivering on expectations. This last step is critical for short-term and long-term income potential. Increase your income potential by simply doing what you said you would do.

Want fans?

Let your yes be yes, your no be no, and your "I will" be "done."

Underpromise and Overdeliver?

Underpromise and overdeliver. You've probably heard this phrase before. The strategy is meant to manage expectations. Set expectations low and then exceed them. The hope is that consistently exceeding expectations will result in happy customers, more referrals, and greater income. Who doesn't like to have their expectations exceeded?

I am going to say (or write) something that many don't say (or write): don't underpromise and overdeliver. A few instances of this happening is fine—even good. But don't make underpromising and overdelivering your long-term gig strategy.

Here's why: consistently adhering to this strategy creates an unrealistic expectation of overdelivering, which you may not always be able to do. This is especially true for side gigs, work that is not your primary job. When overdelivering is the expectation, your customer becomes disappointed when you simply make good on your original agreement.

Don't play the game.

Instead, *deliver on expectations and give them something small and unexpected.* I'll explain that in a moment.

Don't Underpromise but Don't Overpromise

I found what I thought was the perfect Valentine present for my wife. The company, a start-up, created a decorative item I knew my wife would love. I came across the product through a Valentine-themed advertisement. So I ordered it.

And waited.

And waited.

Valentine's Day was quickly approaching, and I was still waiting.

I emailed them. No response. I thought I had been scammed, but, as I researched the company, I noticed that some customers had received their order and loved it.

Others were like me, no product and no response.

I never received an email from them. Eventually, my order arrived—On March 8. Happy Valentine's Day!

It appears that the advertisement was a wild success for them. In fact, it was too successful. They received so many orders they could not deliver on many of them.

They overpromised.

Don't intentionally underpromise, but don't overpromise either. One of the most common ways expectations are not met is through overpromising. Overpromising can come in a variety of forms.

> Overpromising the deadline—saying you will complete the product or service before you are able.
>
> Overpromising the product—saying it will be something greater than it ends up being.
>
> Overpromising the experience—setting expectations for an experience with your service or product that you simply cannot meet.

You should be excited about your side gig. You should want to talk about and promote all the reasons people should consider your side gig. But be careful in your excitement not to promise a deadline, product, or experience you cannot deliver.

This requires having good inventory skills—being able to predict, to the best of your ability, how long you will need to accomplish a task, the quality of the finished work, and the overall experience for the customer. The more organized and realistic you are, the better the chances are that you will neither overpromise nor underpromise.

For step 7, we considered the importance of your calendar and workflows. These are critical tools for delivering on deadline expectations. Before you commit to providing your service or product, map out what it would look like on your calendar. How long will the job take you? When would you be able to put in those hours? When you have mapped out the necessary hours, make sure you maintain them.

Tell people what you are going to do, and do it.

The Power of Reputation

I'm going to assume you have bought something online before. But before you made the purchase, you checked on something—the reviews. You looked at the ratings. On average, how many stars does it receive? You read about individuals' experiences with the product or service you were considering.

If you found positive ratings and reviews, you made the purchase. Or, if you found negative ratings and reviews, you did not make the purchase.

Peer-to-peer reviews are incredibly powerful. For some, peer reviews are more influential than expert reviews. They are from real people who have used the product or service in the real world.

Do you remember the story about my wife posting about built-in bookshelves on our community Facebook page? Do you know what some of the most powerful recommendations were, those we paid attention to most? They were from people who recommended a builder based on their own experience. Some even provided pictures of their bookshelves.

They were fans.

If you are going to increase your income through a side gig, you should care about your reputation. Not only are you representing Christ, but reputation will become one of the influential reasons people choose either to use or not use what you have to offer.

What is one of the best ways to ensure a good reputation?

Deliver on expectations.

And give them something small and unexpected.

Right now, pull out your phone or computer. Read 5-star reviews of some people and businesses offering something similar to you. What do they say? Why are they so happy with the service or product?

Write down a few common themes here.

5-star theme 1 _____

5-star theme 2 _____

5-star theme 3 _____

Now consider what this means for your side gig.

Something Small and Unexpected

I know what you are thinking: *Wait, didn't you just tell me not to underpromise and overdeliver?*

Yes, I did.

But providing something small and unexpected doesn't rise to the level of overdelivering on your promise.

Providing something small and unexpected is a nice touch that makes you stand out from others. In a way, it's promotion. It is the slight nudge that prompts them to give you a good review and tell others about their experience.

It helps create fans.

For Uber and Lyft drivers it's the small bottle of water available to riders and the preparation of numerous musical playlists, ready to play whatever genre the rider prefers.

For the pet sitter it's the daily picture of the pet to the owner just so they know their beloved Lulu is doing well.

For the craft maker, it's the short, handwritten note to thank the purchaser.

For the Airbnb renter, it's the small, locally produced item on the bed's pillow.

For the children's English-as-a-second-language teacher, it's teaching children how to tell their parents they love them.

For every side gig, there is something small and unexpected you can provide your customers.

Providing something small and unexpected is a nice touch that makes you stand out from others.

And it is the small, almost effortless touch your customer will remember and will prompt them to provide positive reviews and recommendations.

Get creative, and consider what small and unexpected thing you can provide your customers.

Take some time and figure out what you can provide your customers that is small and unexpected. Be creative and have fun with it. Go ahead and write down your ideas so you don't forget them.

Idea 1 _____

Idea 2 _____

Idea 3 _____

Create Fans

Consider how you can create fans.

Don't create unrealistic expectations by regularly underpromising and overdelivering. Set appropriate expectations and deliver on them. Provide your customers something small and unexpected. These seemingly simple suggestions will go a long way to help increase your income, not just in the short run but in the long run as well.

Ready, Set, Go *Find More Money!*

You have worked through your *Find More Money* workflow:

     ❑ **Step 1: Know God's Plan for Money**
     ❑ **Step 2: Know God's Plan for Work**
     ❑ **Step 3: Know Your Find More Money Goal**

❑ **Step 4: Know You**
❑ **Step 5: Get a Gig**
❑ **Step 6: Know Your Business**
❑ **Step 7: Get Organized**
❑ **Step 8: Overcommunicate**
❑ **Step 9: Create Fans**

You know God's plan for money and work. You have your Monthly *Find More Money* Goal. You have your side gig. You are organized and ready to overcommunicate. You are prepared to create fans.

Now is the time to hit the launch button. Now is the time to find more money, get financially healthy, and live the generous, kingdom-advancing life God designed you to experience.

You can do this. Let's go.

Find more money.
Get financially healthy.
Advance God's kingdom in your city.

The Job-Gig Relationship

It was Thursday evening. Austin stood in front of Ben's front door. The house was nice, and a new sports car was in the driveway. It looked like Ben had done well in his early career.

Ben opened the door. "Hey, man!" greeted Ben. "It's good to see you."

Austin shook Ben's hand. "Good to see you too, Ben."

After making some small talk, Ben showed Austin the faucet that needed replacing. "This faucet just never worked properly. I think it was a lemon. There's the new one." Ben pointed to a box on the floor.

"No problem," said Austin. "I'm happy to do it."

Austin took a "before" picture and started disassembling the old faucet. "Man, it looks like you are doing well, Ben. You have a great house."

"Thanks," replied Ben. "I just hope we can hold on to it."

Not knowing what Ben meant, Austin laughed. "What do you mean?"

"Well, the mortgage payment is pretty much crushing us. And we just leased that car out front. I don't understand how everyone else affords all this stuff."

Austin put down his tools. "Well, a lot of people can't afford it. They live off debt. And eventually it catches up with them."

Ben put his hand on his head. "Man, I feel like everything is catching up with us." He bit his cheek. "Hey, you're a pastor, right?" questioned Ben.

"I am," said Austin.

"You know me. I've never really been very religious. But can I ask you a question?"

"Of course," approved Austin.

"Our finances are not the only struggles we are facing," Ben said transparently. "Our marriage stinks. And I'm pretty sure we're terrible parents. I don't like who we are, and I know there has to be more. Do you think your God has helped you with this stuff?"

Austin was floored. Usually, once people found out he was a pastor, they either got really awkward or really transparent. And Ben was being the latter.

For the next forty-five minutes, Austin used the faucet replacement as an illustration. "Look, you can try all you want, but until you replace you and your ways with God and his ways, it will never work like you want it to. You will always be disappointed—in your finances, marriage, and parenting."

Ben seemed to listen intently, and Austin finished installing the new faucet. "Works just like it was designed to," Austin smiled.

Before leaving, Austin thought of Sophia, and for some reason her suggestion just seemed right for the moment. Austin took out a piece of paper and wrote the first Bible verse that came to mind, Revelation 21:5.

"Look, I am making everything new."

Austin handed the paper to Ben, and Ben read it. Ben smiled and thanked Austin. They shook hands one more time before Austin left.

As Austin started his car, he couldn't help but think that, maybe, he could use this side gig for something much greater than just making money. He could use it to connect with those who are broken and in need of God's love, those who would never enter a church building on their own, those who would never seek out a pastor but would talk to a handyman working in their house, who happened to be a pastor. What if this side gig helped extend the reach of Little Creek and the church's ministry to the community?

What if . . .

Whatever You Do

"Whatever you do, do it from the heart, as something done for the Lord and not for people, knowing that you will receive the reward of an inheritance from the Lord. You serve the Lord Christ." (Col. 3:23–24)

This verse has significant implications for our work. Why? Because it doesn't provide any exclusions. It doesn't say,

"Whatever you do, unless you don't like your job, do it from the heart."

"Whatever you do, unless you don't like your boss, do it
from the heart."

"Whatever you do, unless your job is not your passion, do it
from the heart."

It definitely doesn't say, "Whatever you do, unless you have
a side gig, do it from the heart."

When we have a job, we are to do it from our heart, as if we
are doing it for the Lord. And when we have a gig, we are still to
do our job from our heart, as if we are doing it for the Lord. But
we are also to do our gig from our heart, as if we are doing it for
the Lord. Which should make us carefully consider the job and gig
relationship.

My friend Sam was a social media guru. He was able to tweet,
post, and snap with the best of them. It was his passion, and he
was really good at it. He took a job as a social media specialist at a
large nonprofit, and he loved working there. But like many college
graduates, Sam and his wife experienced the burden of looming
student loan debt. Money was tight. They wanted to pay off the
debt, but their current income wasn't enough to put a lot of money
toward it. Sam needed to find more money.

Eventually, Sam found quite a few—ten to be exact—other
companies who needed help with their social media, digital
advertising, and websites. But they didn't need a full-time employee.
Some needed ongoing part-time work, and others needed one-off
projects. They contracted Sam to handle their social media and a
few other projects.

Now, was the nonprofit upset about this? Not at all. In fact,
they were thrilled for Sam, and themselves.

Weird, right?

You see, the additional income Sam received from the gigs actually kept him at the nonprofit, as opposed to his having to try to find another job that paid more. When other, higher paying jobs at outside companies were offered, Sam was able to turn them down and stick with the nonprofit he loved. It also exposed him to a variety of challenges in social media, advertising, and web design. These challenges helped him hone his craft.

The gigs made him more valuable, not less valuable, to the nonprofit.

Sam's side gig didn't hinder his ability to do his job as if he were doing it for the Lord. And neither should your gig.

Can Side Gigs Actually Help Your Job?

Here is what many people assume—side gig work hurts primary work. Throwing in a side gig has to diminish your ability to deliver at your main job, right?

It can. But it doesn't have to. In fact, it can be for the good, not just for the side gigger but for the organization for which they work as well.

Side gigs can feed into the success of your job. They can accelerate your performance. They can infuse life into your job. New challenges, fresh ideas, skill improvement, and increased morale resulting from side gigs can make you a better employee.

And that is how you need to be thinking about your gig—as something that can actually help your current job performance.

You don't want to reduce your ability to do well at your current job. Getting fired does

> **Side gigs can feed into the success of your job.**

not help you find more money. As you take on side gigs, you should be asking, "How can I find synergy between my job and my gig?" If you find ways in which synergy exists, you will find yourself being a better employee *and* a better side gigger.

Side Gigs Can Provide New Challenges and Help You Grow as an Employee

Sam learned a lot by working with outside companies. Some of the companies he helped were dramatically different from the nonprofit.

Sam's most consistent gig was with a small fast-food chain that specialized in tacos. Who doesn't like tacos? Apparently, quite a few people. The nonprofit didn't receive many complaints, but this taco chain did. Because of this, Sam became adept at managing social-media complaints and crisis communication. When someone posted a complaint about the nonprofit on social media, Sam handled it with ease.

Side Gigs Can Provide Fresh Ideas and Testing Grounds for Your Current Employer

The small taco chain had one goal—sell more tacos. They were in business to make money, and more tacos meant more money. The taco chain wanted Sam to do some digital advertising in hopes of selling more tacos, and they gave him a pretty large budget to do it. This allowed him not just to sell more tacos (which they did) but also to test different ways of advertising to people.

And guess what? He applied what he learned to the nonprofit, ensuring that the money the nonprofit could put toward advertising did not go to waste.

Side Gigs Can Improve Existing Skills or Cause One to Learn New Skills

Sam has created four or five websites for outside companies. Guess how many he created prior to pursuing gig work?

One.

At some point one company took a chance on Sam, a relatively inexperienced website developer. I guess they assumed that since he could tweet, he could build as well. How different can it be?

Sam did learn how to build a website. Word got out. So he built another one. And another one. And another one. And guess what he could now help the nonprofit do? You guessed it. His new skill became a big help to the nonprofit. They didn't just have a social-media expert. They had a web designer too.

Side Gigs Can Improve Work Morale

Your full-time job may not be one that you are exactly passionate about. Unlike Sam, you would prefer to work somewhere else that aligns with your interests, which can decrease your motivation to do well at work.

A side gig can help. Side gigs become creative outlets for many workers. They aren't able to work in their passion area full-time, so they find a gig that allows them to do it part-time. Knowing they have the opportunity to work in their passion area, even if not full-time, can improve their overall attitude at work. They no longer feel stuck but have outlets where they can engage their passions. They no longer treat their work as if they are stuck and miserable.

In fact, the job can become an important means that allows them to do something in the area of their passions.

Taking on a side gig does not have to be to the detriment of your primary job. In fact, it could enhance your ability to be a better employee.

That's what side gigs did for Sam.

Maybe a side gig can do that for you as well. Find more money *and* become a better employee. Sounds pretty good, huh?

Side Gigs Can Reduce Your Fear of Risk-Taking at Work

I had just finished up a radio interview about following God's design for money when one of the production specialists pulled me aside. He told me to keep spreading the message. It was incredibly encouraging. He went on to tell me how having financial margin reduced his fear of losing his job. With margin and savings, he became an emboldened employee, willing to speak up, be creative, and take wise risks for the company. He became a better employee.

Side gigs can reduce your fear of risk-taking at work because you are not overwhelmed with the fear of losing your job. You've developed margin in your budget, and you know you are still able to generate income to cover you for the time being if you were to lose your job. This confidence in your financial position can mentally free you to become a more creative, contributing employee.

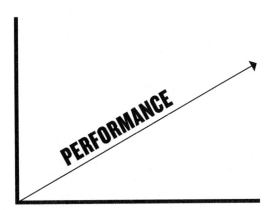

New challenges
Fresh ideas
Skill improvement
Increased morale
+ Reduced fear of risk
_____
Better work performance

Complementary, Not Contradictory Side Gigs

Gig work doesn't have to hurt your job. But let's be real—it can.

Sam was smart in selecting his side gigs. He pursued side gigs that fed into his current job. He chose complementary side gigs and avoided contradictory side gigs. And you need to be able to identify both.

Look, I don't want you to lose your job. I think you would agree with that sentiment. So be careful not to take a gig that puts

> **Gig work doesn't have to hurt your job. But let's be real—it can.**

your current employment at risk. You need a complementary, not a contradictory, side gig.

Complementary side gigs have a hand-and-glove relationship with your current job. They actually fit together quite nicely. They make sense.

Contradictory gigs are like the oil to your job's water. They just don't mix, no matter how hard you try. And it's obvious.

Pursue side gigs that complement your current work, and avoid side gigs that contradict your current work. You want to find side gigs that accelerate your ability to be a good employee, not erode it. It sounds simple, but many find themselves with side gigs that hurt their primary job. And three areas are the most susceptible—visions, customers, and schedules.

Complementary, Not Contradictory Visions

Imagine you work for Nike at their Beaverton, Oregon, headquarters. Your job responsibility is in the sales division, trying to get every person on the planet wearing shoes with a swoosh logo on them. It is a good job, but money is tight. Credit cards and student loan debt suck out any possible margin in your budget. You want to put money toward the debt, but there just isn't any left.

So you decide to become a side gigger. You consider your passion—you love sports. You consider your skills—you know how to sell shoes. And then you find an opportunity—consulting for Adidas's sales division. They want help figuring out how to sell more shoes. You enter into a contract with them for consulting services.

You already see the problem.

Nike wants to be on everyone's feet, and so does Adidas. To help one achieve their vision hurts the other's ability to achieve theirs. The visions and goals are contradictory, not complementary.

Assume the same scenario, but instead of the Adidas side gig, you come across a side gig teaching young basketball players how to improve their skills. (Apparently, you have basketball skills as well. Congratulations, you are multitalented.)

The side gig's vision is to develop basketball players. Suddenly you have a side gig that helps you better understand a segment of your customers—basketball players, which could actually help you make more sales at Nike. The visions are complementary, not contradictory. (Just make sure you're not giving those shoes away for free. You don't want to be the center of the next recruiting scandal.)

You can see how one side gig can hurt your current work while another helps. What's a good way to know whether a job's and gig's visions are complementary or contradictory? Ask this question: Would you be nervous to tell your boss about your side gig?

Sam's gigs did not always have complementary visions (the nonprofit wasn't concerned about tacos), but they definitely weren't contradictory.

Having your company and side gig chasing the same vision and goals is not always a sign that the gig is complementary. In the Nike illustration, both companies wanted the same thing, which meant they were competitors. You were helping the competition.

Does a gig hinder or help your primary company's vision? If the answer is "hinder," you want to stay away from it. If the answer is "help," you should consider going for it.

Complementary, Not Contradictory Customers

This should go without saying, but I'll say it anyway: *it is wrong to steal your company's customers to support your side gig.* If you work for an interior design firm and pull aside one of their customers to whisper in their ear, "I can do the same work for half the cost—here's my number," that is objectively wrong.

I think we can all agree on that. The eighth commandment applies here—don't steal.

If you have complementary, not contradictory visions, it's easier to find complementary customers. Side-gig customers that have no relationship to your primary job are typically complementary, especially if you are not trying to steer them away from your company. In the Nike example, the basketball players were complementary customers. You provided them a service not offered by Nike.

Here is a telling question: Will recommending your side-gig customer to your current company's services or products cause you to lose income?

Why is this question important? As a Nike employee, you could recommend the basketball players to wear Nike shoes, and it would have no impact on your side gig income. Why? Because you have complementary customers. You aren't taking money away from Nike, and they are not taking money away from you. In fact, both your side gig and Nike can potentially make money from your gig customers.

They are complementary.

Sam's side-gig customers didn't compete with those the nonprofit was attempting to reach. The nonprofit wasn't concerned about how many hard-shell chicken tacos people were eating. Now, was Sam able to push consumers of tacos to the nonprofit? Not really. There wasn't much of a connection. And that is okay. Complementary customers are preferred but not necessary.

Pursuing complementary customers will work to your advantage in the long run. And if a side gig that provides complementary customers does not exist, just make sure they are not contradictory customers, where your employer loses customers when the gig wins customers, and vice versa.

Complementary, Not Contradictory Schedules

Side gigs should not interfere with your ability to meet expectations for your primary job. Contradictory schedules erode your ability to do your job well, and they can put your job at risk.

You are exhausted at work because you were up all night working on your gig. You regularly leave work early, missing important meetings, because of your gig. You regularly show up late, starting behind before you even get started, because of your gig. You even sneak in gig work at your regular work without your company's knowledge.

You have contradictory schedules.

Here is another question you need to consider: Would your gig prevent you from meeting job expectations? If the answer is yes, you probably have contradictory schedules.

For Sam, the answer was no.

Were there times when Sam had to respond on social media to an unhappy taco customer during job hours? Sure. But the nonprofit was okay with it because he communicated it, and it did not hinder his ability to meet job expectations. Sam did most of his gig work before and after normal job hours. But social-media conversations never stop. Believe it or not, people complain about tacos during the daytime hours too, not just early morning and late evening hours. The nonprofit understood the nature of the gig, and they thought the benefits of Sam's having the gig (as long as he met job expectations) far outweighed the costs.

If you are stressing about contradictory schedules, let me bring some comfort—many gigs allow for significant schedule flexibility. And it's up to you, the side gigger, to develop a complementary schedule.

More than likely you can find a side-gig schedule that complements your job schedule.

As a Job and a Gig Done for the Lord

God wants us to do everything as if we are doing it for him. This should make us consider the job and gig relationship.

We should do our job as if we are doing it for the Lord.

We should do our gig as if we are doing it for the Lord.

Therefore, we should avoid contradictory relationships, where one is injured by the other.

Complementary relationships allow this to happen. They allow us to pursue excellence with both the job and the gig, which also allows us to be more successful in both finding more money and working as if we are working for the Lord.

Find more money.
Get financially healthy.
Advance God's kingdom in your state.

When Does a Side Gig Turn into a Full-Time Gig?

Friday was Austin's day off. The weather was incredible, so he and Brooklyn went to Oak City Park to walk around.

"What a day!" exclaimed Brooklyn. "This weather is incredible."

Austin took a deep breath of the warming, North Carolina air. "Aah."

Austin held Brooklyn's hand as they walked. The couple discussed his time with Ben and how both of them hoped the side gig could open up future ministry opportunities.

"But," said Austin, transitioning to their current reality, "We need money now. I have no idea how long it will take to get steady side-gig work as a handyman. So I'm going to put the handyman gig on hold and plug into an existing service, like driving people around."

"No shopping?" jokingly questioned Brooklyn. Admittedly, she was a little bummed that the gig didn't work out, but she agreed with his decision.

"Not if I want to make money," smiled Austin.

They passed one of the park's playgrounds. Kids were running around everywhere. They both thought of their son, quietly smiled, and held each other's hand a little more tightly.

Suddenly, Austin's phone buzzed. He looked at the phone. He had a new email with the subject line reading "HELP!" Curious, Austin opened the email.

Austin stopped walking.

"What is it?" questioned Brooklyn. "Is everything okay?"

Just then, his phone buzzed again. Another email. This time the subject line read, "Repairs needed."

"Yes, everything is fine," answered Austin. "Apparently, Ben posted my before and after pictures on social media. He also included a picture of the verse I wrote out for him, and gave me a great recommendation."

Austin's phone buzzed again—another handyman request.

"I guess Ben is a pretty trusted guy when it comes to recommendations," said Austin as he opened the next email. "This is incredible."

Brooklyn leaned up to Austin and looked at the emails. Brooklyn was excited for her husband.

"So, are you still going to do the ride-share thing?" She asked a question to which she already knew the answer.

"Um . . . I don't think so." The phone buzzed again. Another request. Austin smiled. "Not sure I'll have time."

"Maybe you could just become a career handyman," Brooklyn said, also knowing he would never do that.

Austin put the phone back in his pocket. "And miss out on what God is doing at Little Creek? No way."

Brooklyn put her arm around Austin.

Austin continued, "We still have a long road ahead of us, but I hope this side gig turns into something that doesn't just allow us to hit those Money Milestones but to be even more generous to our church. What if God used our resources and our small church to advance his kingdom in Raleigh and beyond?"

Brooklyn smiled. She liked that thought.

Going Full-Time

I recently ran across the story of a woman named Melanie.[1]

Melanie needed some additional income, so her friend recommended Rover.com, a service I've referenced a few times already. She already had two dogs, and Melanie liked the idea of having other dogs around for them to play with. So she set up her account and waited.

Melanie began to get requests for her service. And, apparently, her customers were pleased with the service they received, as they continued to reach out to her the next time they needed pet sitting.

Repeat and new clients began to fill her schedule, sometimes booking her service several weeks out. Eventually, Melanie was receiving enough income through pet sitting to make it her full-time job. Melanie's side gig is now her full-time gig.

What If?

You didn't jump into the gig economy to find a job. You wanted a side gig, something to supplement the income from your job. Your challenge was not just on the expense side of the financial equation but also on the income side. You were living paycheck to paycheck, maybe unable to pay the bills, unable to put money toward debt, unable to save money for retirement.

You set out to find more money. And you found it. Your income has increased.

But something else happened. You found the trifecta—the place where passion, skill, and opportunity meet. And you found yourself really enjoying the work. You think you have found it—the type of work you were meant to do.

So you want to do more of it. You want to commit more time to the side gig. In fact, you're wondering if this side gig can take the place of your job. At first the idea seems outrageous, but your mind keeps pumping out the same question: What if?

What if you could make it work? What if it actually happened? What if?

And then "what if" turns to "how and when?"

How do I know I can make it work? When is the right time to make the jump?

Those who find a side gig they love inevitably begin to wonder whether they can go full-time with their gig. I hope you find yourself in this position—loving your side gig so much you desire to go full-time with it. But loving your side gig is not enough of an indicator that you are ready to make the jump.

You need more than enjoyment.

So here are five signs that indicate you might consider turning your side gig into a full-time gig.

Sign 1: The Side Gig Has Proved to Be Enduring

If you are going to leave your job for your side gig, you need to be confident your side gig will be there in six months or a year.

To determine whether your side gig will last, consider two common reasons side gigs eventually cease—fads and competition.

Fads: In college, I spent two summers in California. And since I was out there, I figured I'd learn to surf. It is what all Californians do, right? I wasn't a great, or even a good, surfer. On most occasions, I would almost drown. But on a rare occasion, I would catch a small wave. It was an incredible experience, standing on top of the water, getting pushed toward the shore. Once I caught the wave, there wasn't much else I needed to do (other than not fall off); the wave did the hard work for me.

Sometimes side gigs find success through fads. A fad is a short-lived craze. They are quickly adopted and then quickly abandoned. Beanie Babies, bell bottoms, and The Macarena—all fads. Fads move forward, seemingly with little effort, like riding a wave. But while the forward movement is easy, eventually the wave suddenly crashes down. The fad is gone.

Side giggers who sell products are most susceptible to fads, especially those side gigs based on selling specific products. Those who used to buy and sell Beanie Babies for a profit are no longer in business. Closets are still filled with tiny bears because the craze quickly faded.

Does your side gig have fad-like characteristics? Did the area in which your side gig resides experience an out-of-nowhere, meteoric rise in popularity? Is there little practical value to what is provided? If so, you may need to keep your regular job.

Question to consider: Does my side gig have fad-like characteristics?

Competition: Competition can also play a major role in your side gig's ability to stand the test of time. You need to provide a reason for people to pay for your product or service instead of paying for another company's similar product or service.

This is often done by cost or differentiation. Let's assume your side gig is selling handmade cowboy hats. To get someone to buy your cowboy hat instead of another, similar cowboy hat, you could sell your hat for less money.

Lower price isn't always possible. And if not cost, you must consider differentiation.

Differentiation is the additional value you provide the customer that your competitors do not. It's what makes your cowboy hats stand out from the rest. Maybe your hats are made of a felt not available to other hat makers. Maybe your cowboy hats have a cupholder on them (note: not a good idea). If you cannot compete on price, your cowboy hats must offer something other cowboy hats do not.

Are you able to compete? Are you able to offer something similar at a lower price? Or are you able to add value your competitors do not? If you can answer yes to one of these questions, you might have the makings of a full-time job on your hands.

Question to consider: Can I compete?

Sign 2: You Are Repeatedly Saying No Because of Capacity Issues

An important indicator of ongoing success is your inability to meet demand.

You are saying no on a regular basis. People are asking for your services, but you simply don't have the time to say yes to every order or request. You are consistently turning down customers.

If this is you, figure out how much additional income you could make if you were to say yes to all requests. Keep track of all of your requests for thirty days. Then calculate the income you would have received if you had the capacity to deliver on those requests.

If the amount of income is substantial, you may be another step closer to transitioning your side gig into a full-time job.

Write down how many times you said "no" in the last thirty days: _____

Write down how much income those requests would have provided: _____

Sign 3: The Finances Make Sense

First, are you financially healthy? Have you been able to pay off your debt and save money? I typically don't recommend someone leaving their job for a gig until they have accomplished Money Milestone 5, having at least three to six months of living expenses saved. Your personal finances will need to get you through any difficult times that arise while perusing your gig full-time.

Second, is the income you receive from the gig substantial enough to support you? For some, their job not only includes a salary but benefits as well—health, retirement, life insurance, etc. Calculate what it truly looks like to support yourself. What are your expenses? How much does health insurance cost outside of the company plan?

Make sure you are financially healthy and that the gig's income is enough to support your living expenses. If the finances make sense, you might be able to go full-time.

Sign 4: You Know How to Scale

Scaling is simply making your side gig larger. As it stands, you are probably able to manage your gig. But the current size of the side gig will probably not be enough to financially support you.

If you want to go full-time, you will need to grow your gig. And this is not as easy as it sounds. Growing your gig means saying yes to more requests, but there is more to it than just that.

Just like your personal finances, there are two sides to your gig's finances—revenue and expenses. You will need to find ways to increase the revenue while keeping the growth in expenses minimized. This will give you more income.

Scaling will require you to work hard and wear a lot of different hats. So, before you make the jump, develop a plan to scale. Write out your plan to grow the gig and increase the revenue while minimizing the expenses.

If you have a good plan to scale the gig, you may be ready to go.

Sign 5: You Are the Right Person to Be Your Boss

Not everyone is ready to be their own boss. Not everyone is wired to be their own boss. That isn't a criticism. Some need a person other than themselves guiding and pushing them. If you are considering going full-time with your gig, you need to know whether you are someone who needs a boss.

When you make the jump to full-time work with your gig, you are your own boss. But how do you know you are ready to be your own boss? Here are a few questions to consider before making the jump:

Do you have a vision for the gig's future? You know where you are going with the gig. Knowing how to scale the gig is part of this. But you also need to have an idea of what you want the future to look like for the gig.

So, do you have a vision for the gig? If so, go ahead and write it out below.

My Vision for the Gig

_____

_____

_____

Are you self-motivated to work hard? Hard work has been a theme in this book and for good reason. A side gig is hard work. It takes effort and intentionality. When you go full-time, the level of effort and intentionality needed rises dramatically. You don't have anyone encouraging you, pushing you to dig deep and work hard. When you are your own boss, _you_ have to push _you_. You have to encourage you. You must be self-motivated to work hard.

Are you okay with hard decisions? You may have contract decisions, promotion decisions, and expense decisions. And while you are making these decisions for your side gig now, new weight will attach to these decisions when you go full-time. The stakes are significantly higher. And you cannot be paralyzed with indecision. You must act. Being your own boss requires you to be comfortable with hard decisions.

Are you okay with difficult obstacles? When you are your own boss, challenges will come your way. There won't be anybody else to help you face them. You won't have a boss telling you that you can do it, that they have your back, or will lead you through the difficulty. Being your own boss requires determination, persistence, and the ability to view obstacles as great opportunities to grow yourself and your business.

Do you know you don't know enough? Harry S. Truman said, "Not all readers are leaders, but all leaders are readers." The best bosses have a humility about them. They are willing to admit they don't know everything, that they have room to grow and learn. They read books, watch educational videos, and talk to people who know what they want to learn. They seek mentors and save money for conferences and other helpful learning experiences. They own their own development.

If you're going full-time with a gig, learning must be a constant. You need to know you don't know enough. You need to own your own development.

Cannonball!

Some will make the jump from side gig to full-time gig. They will leave their job and totally immerse themselves in the gig economy.

Most will not. And that's okay. Many side gigs simply don't translate well to full-time work. You have not failed at your side gig if it never turns into a full-time business.

But if you're itching to turn your side gig into a full-time gig, be thoughtful about it. Make sure you and your gig are ready to make the jump.

Find more money.
Get financially healthy.
Advance God's kingdom in your country.

The Mind-Set for Finding More Money

It was Saturday again. Austin was amazed at how everything had changed from last Saturday. Last Saturday he and Brooklyn felt hopeless. This Saturday they were full of hope. Last Saturday they were consistently on the verge of arguing. This Saturday they were consistently on the verge of celebrating. Last Saturday they were looking at a bill they could not afford. This Saturday they were both looking at opportunities to find more money. They both knew the road ahead was long, but they felt miles from where they once were.

Austin was standing outside of Cary's house. He had just finished working at a house in Cary's neighborhood so he wanted to stop by. He rang the doorbell, and after a moment Cary opened the door.

"Hey, Austin!" greeted Cary. "Good to see you. What brings you to the house?"

"You won't believe it, but I have two jobs today," Austin said enthusiastically.

Cary unexpectedly lunged at Austin and gave him a bear hug. "I knew it!" Cary said.

"Okay, you can let go. . . . Need to breathe." Cary let go. Once Austin caught his breath, he said, "Thanks. We're excited too."

Austin could hear footsteps running down the hallway and toward the door. Suddenly, Sophia appeared at the door, smiling as always.

"Hey, Pastor Austin!" said Sophia.

"Hey, Sophia," replied Austin.

"Have you hit your money goal yet?" Sophia abruptly questioned.

Austin chuckled. "Well, no. Not yet. But I think that by the end of today, we will only need $7,000 more."

Sophia pulled out her notebook. She quickly jotted something down. "That means you only have $1,000 more for this month."

"That's right," responded Austin.

Just then he remembered why he stopped by in the first place. "Hey, I just want to say thank you. Thank you for introducing me to the world of side gigs, Cary. And thank you, Sophia, for the Bible verse idea. God is already using it."

Sophia gave a proud smile.

"We're grateful for you, Austin," said Cary. "We know you love our church, and we are glad you are staying. Maybe one day we can pay you more, and you won't need a side gig."

Just then Austin's phone buzzed. But it wasn't an email from a potential new client. It was a text from an old one. Austin read the text.

"Hey, Austin. It's Ben. Are you cool if our family goes to your church tomorrow?"

Austin then looked back at Cary. "Believe it or not, I'm not in any rush to get rid of this side gig. I'm going to work hard, trust God, and allow him to use the gig and the money I earn to reach people like Ben, in our community and beyond."

Austin replied to Ben's text.

"We'd love to have you. See you tomorrow."

———————

What It Takes

As I talk to people who have increased their income in the gig economy, I've noticed many similarities. Those who seem to get the most out of their side gig have a similar mind-set. They expect hard work, and they trust God. They are patient, persistent, habitual, willing to fail, and have fun. Let's look at each one.

They Expect Hard Work

Time, energy, and money.

All three are finite. A side gigger knows this well.

You only have so much time you can put toward your side gig. You still have a job. You still have a family. You still have your relationship with God. All require time. To do one is to take time away from the other.

We all have only so much energy to give. Eventually the coffee loses it effect, the Red Bull wings get clipped. Mental and physical energy are not always present. Expending energy on one task means less energy for the next task.

You already know that money is finite. Your bank account reflects this. Spending money eating out means you cannot spend that money on something else. But side giggers are not just aware that their money is finite. They are aware that others' money is finite as well. This means that other people, like the side gigger, must determine how to use their money. They have to know where to spend and where not to spend.

What does understanding the finiteness of time, energy, and money do for the side gigger?

They know that at times side-gig work will be hard. There will be moments when they don't feel like working. There will be moments when their energy is low. But they must push through and provide value to the customer because the customer doesn't have to spend money; they decide to.

Side gigs can be fun. They can be a place where your passion and skill meet. But even when the work is enjoyable, effort is still needed. Increasing one's income usually doesn't happen without effort.

Side giggers are willing to put in the work. They expect it. They have a hard-work mind-set.

They Trust God

Whether you experience an increase in income or no increase at all, you can easily find yourself moving away from relying on God's provision.

According to 1 Timothy 6:17, those who are financially successful are susceptible to arrogance. They may start attributing their success to their intellect, their drive, their experience, or their creativity. And while they may voice the need for God in their real life and work, their life and work point to something else—*themselves*.

At the same time those who experience times of financial disappointment, when income doesn't increase as hoped, can also find themselves drifting away from reliance on God's provision.

Because he didn't provide in a way they had hoped, they stop treating him as the Provider and turn their attention to themselves.

High levels of anger and stress can be an indicator that you have moved away from relying on God to provide. You are angry because the income did not materialize this month. You are stressed because you have placed the entire burden of increasing your income on your own shoulders.

As a side gigger, you need to be of the hardworking mind-set. But you also need to be of the reliance mind-set. You must trust him.

Whether God provides much or little, remember the words of Jesus in Luke 11:11–13:

> "What father among you, if his son asks for a fish, will give him a snake instead of a fish? Or if he asks for an egg, will give him a scorpion? If you then, who are evil, know how to give good gifts to your children, how much more will the heavenly Father give the Holy Spirit to those who ask him!"

Our God is a good Father. He is our Provider. We can trust that, as we work hard, whatever he provides is exactly what we need.

They Are Patient

Some side gigs produce income faster than others. Whether you are an opportunity taker or an opportunity maker, there is often an initial period of slow, gradual increase in income. Undoubtedly, you want your side gig to have a rocket-like launch—moving from gravity to weightlessness in a matter of minutes. And it could happen. But it is not most side giggers' experience. Their experience is more like the taking off of an airplane, gradually going from the ground to "you are now free to move about the cabin."

In the gig economy, there is value in patience. There is value in simply being patient with finding a side gig. And there is value in allowing the time needed for a side gig to take off.

> Our God is a good Father. He is our Provider. We can trust that, as we work hard, whatever he provides is exactly what we need.

If you are working hard and trusting God with the results, be patient.

They Are Persistent

Most of us have had cars that struggle to start. You turn the key and the engine starts whining, like a child you are attempting to wake from a nap. You can almost hear your car whine, "But I don't want to." But after a few more attempts, the car gives in and its engine roars to life.

Side gigs can be like that. If you set the gig aside for a while, it becomes difficult to get it roaring back to life. But it's not the gig's fault. You are the engine. You are what makes the gig go.

How do you prevent this from occurring? You keep the engine running.

To maintain momentum in your side gig, you must engage it on an almost daily basis. So as a side gigger, you should attempt to do one gig-related action every day (except when you take an intentional break from job and side gig).

The action doesn't need to be significant. Maybe you answer a few emails. Maybe you update your profile. Maybe you create one post for your Facebook community page. Or maybe you respond to someone else's post.

Certainly you can take significant action. If you are a driver, you can get in your car and take someone to their destination. If you are a handyman, you can go fix something at somebody's house (assuming you have an appointment).

The key is to do something, to keep the engine running. This will keep the side-gig momentum going for you, which can lead to increased income.

They Are Habitual

You already have habits. Some are good and others are bad. Some you are aware of, and others you are oblivious to. For those of you who are married, you have some habits you didn't know you had until your spouse asked you, "Why do you do that?" And then you realized you had a habit.

Over time you can develop new habits—both good and bad. And while bad habits are usually easy to create, developing good habits requires work. Successful side giggers are known for their good habits. They work hard to develop life patterns that accelerate their ability to find more money. You can do the same.

Let me share with you a few habits of successful side giggers.

Wake up early. Many side giggers get a lot accomplished before they ever leave the house. They devote a portion of their morning to their gig. They wake up early, before the kids get up, and focus on their gig. They find that the quiet, uninterrupted early morning hours are perfect for their gigs.

If you are not a morning person, let me encourage you—neither was I. I tried a few times to regularly wake up early, but it never took. I would wake up early for a few days, but I couldn't turn it into a habit.

So I just assumed God made me a night owl and I could do little about it.

Then I read an article that said whether we are a morning person or a night owl was not based on genetics. It was something one could change. Admittedly, I don't remember the science behind the argument, so if you are a scientist or read articles to the contrary, don't get mad at me. All I know is that the article motivated me to give it one more try.

And by doing so, I found my wake-up hack—exercise classes.

Most gyms offer some type of exercise class as soon as they open. I signed up for a spin class. I'd never done one before so I decided to give it a shot. And that was all it took. I knew they were expecting me, which forced me to get out of bed and out the door. It also forced me to go to bed earlier, knowing I had to get up early.

After about three weeks I had a new habit—waking up early (and going to bed early). The early morning hours were no longer a struggle for me. Instead, I looked forward to them. Because if I wasn't at the gym, I had the house seemingly all to myself. And for a side gigger, this is an ideal time to get work done.

Not every gig has work that can be accomplished in the morning. You might not be able to deliver groceries at 5:30 a.m. But even if you cannot work on your gig in the early morning hours, get other things done so you can free up other parts of the day. Exercise, read, email, plan. Leverage your morning hours.

Sleep. Wake up early. But get your sleep. God created you to sleep. Historically, operating on little sleep was perceived as a strength. Now, we know too much about the importance of sleep. Most people need seven to nine hours of sleep. You need it for your mental and physical health. You also need sleep for your job and gig. Adequate sleep helps your productivity, memory, creativity, and social interactions—all important for your job and gig.

If you decide to wake up early, make sure to develop a good bedtime routine. And even when you don't feel tired, maintain the routine. Just as you must force yourself to get out of bed, you will have to force yourself to get into bed, at least initially.

Get some sleep.

Check your progress. How do you know whether you are close to hitting your monthly money goal? You check your progress. Successful side giggers regularly check the results of their work, the amount of money made. I recommend doing this daily—not because you are obsessed with making money but because you need to know how to manage your day, week, and month.

A simple daily check-in will tell you if you need to work more hours to achieve your goal. It can also tell you whether the gig is working for you, that you are making the money you hoped to make. If not, you may need to find another gig. The only way to know how to plan for the future is to have a good grasp on your present reality.

Check your progress.

They Are Okay with Failing, but They Are Not Okay with Giving Up

Thomas Edison once said, "I have not failed. I've just found ten thousand ways that won't work." I love this quote, and it rings true for many side giggers.

Opportunity takers will try gigs that do not deliver the income for which you had hoped. Maybe your town isn't a real destination for Airbnb renters. Maybe there aren't many dogs that need sitting.

For opportunity makers, not every attempt will gain traction. Not every idea will meet a need for which people are willing to pay. Not enough people will purchase your hand-carved Christmas ornaments. Reselling sports gear may not be a home run.

When faced with disappointment, remember this—it is okay to fail. You have permission. But it isn't okay to give up.

You started this journey for a reason—to take a step toward financial health for the sake of living and giving generously. You need to pay your bills. You need to pay off your debt. You need to use your resources to advance God's kingdom. If the income side of the equation is where your financial challenge finds its remedy, you must not give up. You must move forward and try again.

I've met many people the world would deem successful—presidents, CEOs, self-made millionaires. And they all have had the shared experience of failure. Each and every one.

Do you know what failure reveals? You did something. You made an attempt. You tried. And that is not something to quit over. It is something for which you should be proud, proud enough to do it again.

Sometimes we let our failures define us. We think that because we could not make it work we are somehow labeled as failures. We are not. You are not.

Your identity is first and foremost found in Christ. And while you may not have experienced success in this venture, your identity remains unchanged.

You can proceed, anchoring your identity in Christ, taking another chance on a gig. Learn from your prior experience, and make yourself better prepared to find more money.

It's okay to fail.

It's not okay to give up.

To find more money, you need this mind-set.

They Have Fun

I was on a treadmill at the gym. On the treadmill next to me was Billy. I noticed that Billy was reading a financial book, and so I asked him about it. As it turns out, Billy used to have a lot of debt, and his regular job did not provide enough income to pay down the debt at a speed he wanted.

Sound familiar?

He started working for Lyft, a ride-share company, to make side income. Everything was going well. He then received an offer to take on a more traditional, hourly, part-time job. So he quit Lyft.

Shortly after he was back with Lyft. I asked him why he went back. Billy's answer wasn't incredibly surprising. He said that the traditional part-time started to feel like work. With Lyft, even though he was working, it never felt burdensome.

Billy now makes $1,000 per month in additional income. Billy is knocking out his debt and enjoying his gig.

Are there times when you need to take an opportunity, even if it is one you don't necessarily enjoy? Sure. But the most successful side giggers find gigs they enjoy overall. This doesn't mean they don't work hard or have difficult moments to work through. But, in general, they like what they are doing.

Live Generously

You picked up this book because you needed more money. You needed margin in your finances. You had bills to pay. You had debt to crush. You had a child's college education or a retirement to fund.

Your lack of money and margin were preventing you from taking that next step in your financial picture. Your lack of money and margin were preventing you from experiencing God's design for you and your money.

More money is not the end. Margin is not the end. Financial health is not the end. They are the means. They are the means that can get us to the point where we are better able to live the generous life for which God has designed us.

Find more money and pay your bills.

Find more money and crush your debt.

Find more money and set up your emergency fund.

Find more money and save for retirement.

Find more money and get financially healthy.

Find more money because financial health is a means through which you can live with your hands open, ready to give and go as God leads you.

Find more money because you are less concerned about financial health and more concerned about reaching your community and the world for Christ.

Find more money because financial health will allow you to say yes as opposed to "not yet."

It is time to find more money. It is time to get financially healthy, but not just for the sake of being financially healthy. It is time for you to live and give generously, leveraging your newfound financial heath to advance God's kingdom to the ends of the earth.

Find more money.
Get financially healthy.
Advance God's kingdom around the
world.

Tomorrow

Austin and Brooklyn were talking quietly with Cary and Sophia back at their small townhouse. The townhouse was a slight mess, but no one seemed to care.

Suddenly, Sophia heard what she had been waiting for—the cry of a newborn baby boy.

Austin and Brooklyn were sitting on their couch. With one hand Austin held Brooklyn's hand. With the other hand, he held a baby rattle. They shared a smile with one another and then looked at Sophia. It had been more than five months since Austin and Brooklyn were sitting on that same couch, with Austin holding a bill instead of a baby rattle.

"It sounds like someone is awake," said Brooklyn to Sophia with a big grin.

Sophia jumped up in excitement.

"You can go with me to get him," said Austin.

Austin and Sophia went into the baby's room. After a quick diaper change, Austin emerged with the baby, Sophia right by his side.

Sophia sat down on the couch, and Austin gently placed the baby in her arms. This was the moment Sophia had been waiting for.

"Little Raleigh is so cute!" gushed Sophia.

Austin and Brooklyn had decided to keep the family tradition alive by naming him Raleigh.

Just then the doorbell rang. Brooklyn yelled for them to come in. The door opened. It was Ben, his wife Holly, and their son Jake.

"Jake!" yelled Sophia. "Come see Raleigh!" Sophia and Jake knew each other from school.

Everyone welcomed the family in. Ben and Holly had been attending church ever since Austin replaced their faucet. They had both placed their faith in Jesus and had been baptized. They were pursuing God's design for their life, including their finances.

"We sold the house!" celebrated Ben. "Time to get a mortgage payment we can afford!"

Everyone cheered.

Austin went to make a bottle for Raleigh in the kitchen area. As he put the bottle together, he watched the room, filled with excitement. They hit their $7,500 goal. But the delivery was less costly than expected—$5,000. They set aside $1,500 for Milestone 2 and gave the remaining $1,000 to Little Creek. It was the largest gift they had ever given as a couple. And they loved it.

Brooklyn was able to stop her side gig because Austin's handyman side gig provided enough income. He had more than enough clients. The income allowed the couple to pursue the Milestones and chase the generous life they knew God wanted them to live. The relationships with his clients allowed Austin and Little Creek's ministry to expand. So far, four clients and their families now attended Little Creek.

That Saturday five months ago was difficult. That Saturday five months ago, Austin was fearful of what the next day would bring. But today he couldn't wait for tomorrow. Because tomorrow was Sunday. Tomorrow his teenagers gathered, and he would point them to Jesus. Tomorrow was another day to advance God's kingdom. Today Austin was ready for tomorrow.

Notes

When Cutting Your Budget No Longer Cuts It

1. "Report on the Economic Well-Being of U.S. Households in 2017," May 2018), Board of Governors of the Federal Reserve System, accessed March 2019, https://www.federalreserve.gov/publications/files/2017-report-economic-well-being-us-households-201805.pdf.

2. Clarie Tsosie and Erin El Issa, "2018 American Household Credit Card Debt Study," NerdWallet.com, December 10, 2018, accessed March 2019, https://www.nerdwallet.com/blog/average-credit-card-debt-household.

3. Kyle Morgan, "Car Loan Statistics," Finder.com, accessed March 2019, https://www.finder.com/car-loan-statistics.

4. Zach Friedman, "Student Loan Debt Statistics in 2019: A $1.5 Trillion Crisis," *Forbes*, February 25, 2019, accessed March 2019, https://www.forbes.com/sites/zackfriedman/2019/02/25/student-loan-debt-statistics-2019/#38ccc826133f.

5. Tara Siegel Bernard, "'Too Little Too Late': Bankruptcy Booms among Older Americans," *The New York Times*, August 5, 2018, accessed March 2019, https://www.nytimes.com/2018/08/05/business/bankruptcy-older-americans.html.

6. Zach Friedman, "78% of Workers Live Paycheck to Paycheck," *Forbes*, January 11, 2019, accessed March 2019, https://www.forbes.com/sites/zackfriedman/2019/01/11/live-paycheck-to-paycheck-government-shutdown/#d41e58a4f10b.

7. TJ McCue, "57 Million U.S. Workers Are Part of the Gig Economy," *Forbes*, April 31, 2018, accessed July 2019, https://www.forbes.com/sites/tjmccue/2018/08/31/57-million-u-s-workers-are-part-of-the-gig-economy/#5e6c57897118.

8. Amanda Dixon, "The Average Side Hustler Earns over $8K Annually," Bankrate.com, June 25, 2018, accessed March 2019, https://www.bankrate.com/personal-finance/smart-money/side-hustles-survey-june-2018.

Step 1: Know God's Plan for Money

1. www.globalrichlish.com

2. Randy Alcorn, *The Treasure Principle* (Portland, OR: Multnomah Books, 2005).

3. James D. Wise, *Inheritolatry* (Maitland, FL: Xulon Press, 2017).

4. "Managing Millennial Money," PWC, accessed July 2019, https://www.pwc.com/us/en/industries/financial-services/library/managing-millennial-money.html.

5. International Mission Board, imb.org.

Step 2: Know God's Plan for Work

1. Gordon Waddell and A. Kim Burton, "Is Work Good for Your Health and Well-being?" The Stationary Office, 2006, accessed March 2019, https://assets.publishing.service.gov.uk/government/uploads/system/uploads/attachment_data/file/214326/hwwb-is-work-good-for-you.pdf.

2. Elizabeth Fernandez, "Not Retiring Comes with a Bonus: Better Health," nbcnews.com, July 30, 2009, accessed March 2019, http://www.nbcnews.com/id/32188496/ns/health-aging/t/not-retiring-comes-bonus-better-health/#.XJE7Gy2ZNuV.

Step 3: Know Your Find More Money Goal

1. Art Rainer, *The Money Challenge: 30 Days of Discovering God's Design for You and Your Money* (Nashville, TN: B&H Publishing, 2017).

Step 4: Know You

1. Art Rainer, *The Marriage Challenge: A Finance Guide for Married Couples* (Nashville, TN: B&H Publishing, 2018).

Step 5: Getting a Gig

1. Chris Guillebeau, "British Man Earns $700/Month Writing Fish Tank Reviews," *Side Hustle School*, podcast audio, retrieved from https://sidehustleschool.com/episode/side-business-writing-fish-tank-reviews.

2. Chris Guillebeau, "Airbnb for Dogs: Woman Hosts Pets at Her Home for $200/Day," *Side Hustle School*, podcast audio, retrieved from https://sidehustleschool.com/episode/dog-airbnb.

3. Chris Guillebeau, "GE Engineer Sells Hand-Crafted Slate Artwork to All 50 States," *Side Hustle School*, podcast audio, retrieved from https://sidehustleschool.com/episode/33.

4. Chris Guillebeau, "How One Man Used a $100 Microphone to Make over $8,000," *Side Hustle School*, podcast audio, retrieved from https://sidehustleschool.com/episode/100-microphone-voice-over-fiverr.

5. Hayden Field, "The Top 10 Side Gigs for 2019 (Infographic)," Enrepreneur.com, January 19, 2019, accessed March 2019, https://www.entrepreneur.com/article/326438.

6. "Wal Mart Cashier Hourly Pay," Glassdoor.com, May 25, 2019, accessed August 26, 2019, https://www.glassdoor.com/Hourly-Pay/Walmart-Wal-Mart-Cashier-Hourly-Pay-E715_D_KO8,24.htm.

7. "How Much Do Pizza Delivery Jobs Pay per Hour?," ZipRecruiter, accessed August 26, 2019, https://www.ziprecruiter.com/Salaries/How-Much-Does-a-Pizza-Delivery-Make-an-Hour.

8. "How Much Do Lyft Drivers Make?," Ridesharedriversapp.com, accessed March 2019, https://rideshareapps.com/how-much-do-lyft-drivers-make.

9. "10 Reasons Why People Choose to Be Shipt Shoppers," Shipt. com, accessed March 2019, https://www.shipt.com/blog/10-reasons -why-people-choose-to-be-shipt-shoppers.

10. Retrieved from https://www.glassdoor.com/Salary/Grubhub -Salaries-E419089.htm.

11. Retrieved from https://flex.amazon.com/faqs.

12. Due to the constantly changing and growing nature of the gig economy, it's likely that some of these will have changed by the time you're reading this book, and that countless more will have been created.

Step 6: Know Your Business

1. Bobby McFerrin, "Don't Worry, Be Happy."

Step 7: Get Organized

1. Charles E. Hummel, *Tyranny of the Urgent* (Downers Grove, IL: IVP Books, 1994).

2. "American Time Use Survey Summary," Bureau of Labor Statistics, June 19, 2019, accessed March 2019, https://www.bls.gov/ news.release/atus.nr0.htm.

Step 8: Overcommunicate

1. Carolanne Mangles, "Search Engine Statistics 2018," smartin- sights.com, January 30, 2019, accessed March 2019, https://www.smart insights.com/search-engine-marketing/search-engine-statistics.

When Does a Side Gig Turn into a Full-Time Gig?

1. Melanie Lockert, "5 Entrepreneurs Who Took Their Side Hustle Full-Time," the balancesmb.com, August 2, 2018, accessed March 2019, https://www.thebalancesmb.com/entrepreneurs-taking -side-hustles-full-time-4136679.

In *The Money Challenge: 30 Days of Discovering God's Design for You and Your Money*, Art Rainer takes you on a journey to financial health. But it is not simply for the sake of financial health. *The Money Challenge* was written to help you experience God's design for you and your finances.

THE MONEY CHALLENGE

30 DAYS OF DISCOVERING GOD'S DESIGN FOR YOU AND YOUR MONEY

ART RAINER

THE MARRIAGE CHALLENGE

A FINANCE GUIDE FOR MARRIED COUPLES

ART RAINER

In *The Marriage Challenge: A Finance Guide for Married Couples*, financial expert and author of *The Money Challenge* Art Rainer takes you on a journey to a financially healthy marriage. Get started on the right foot, or get back on the right track, by accepting the challenge and realizing God's design for money and marriage.

B&H PUBLISHING

Don't miss **ANY** of the Secret Slide agents' adventures!